West African Women in the Diaspora

This book examines fictional works by women authors who have left their homes in West Africa and now live as members of the diaspora.

In recent years, a compelling array of critically acclaimed fiction by women in the West African diaspora has shifted the direction of the African novel away from post-colonial themes of nationhood, decolonization, and cultural authenticity, and towards explorations of the fluid and shifting constructions of identity in transnational spaces. Drawing on works by Chimamanda Ngozi Adichie, Buchi Emecheta, Ama Ata Aidoo, Sefi Atta, Chika Unigwe, and Taiye Selasi, this book interrogates the ways in which African diaspora women's fiction portrays the realities of otherness, hybridity, and marginalized existence of female subjects beyond Africa's borders. Overall, the book demonstrates that life in the diaspora is an uncharted journey of expanded opportunities along with paradoxical realities of otherness.

Providing a vivid and composite portrait of African women's experiences in the diasporic landscape, this book will be of interest to researchers of migration and diaspora topics, and African, women's, and world literature.

Rose A. Sackeyfio is Associate Professor in the Department of Liberal Studies at Winston-Salem State University, USA.

African Diaspora Literary and Cultural Studies

Literary Black Power in the Caribbean
Fiction, Music and Film
Rita Keresztesi

Cultural Mobilities Between Africa and the Caribbean
Edited by Birgit Englert, Barbara Gföllner and Sigrid Thomsen

Oral Forms of Nigerian Autobiography and Life Stories
Adetayo Alabi

Transnational Africana Women's Fictions
Edited by Cheryl Sterling

West African Women in the Diaspora
Narratives of Other Spaces, Other Selves
Rose A. Sackeyfio

Black Women's Literature of the Americas
Griots and Goddesses
Tonia Leigh Wind

For more information about this series, please visit: www.routledge.com/African-Diaspora-Literary-and-Cultural-Studies/book-series/ADLCS

West African Women in the Diaspora
Narratives of Other Spaces, Other Selves

Rose A. Sackeyfio

LONDON AND NEW YORK

First published 2022
by Routledge
2 Park Square, Milton Park, Abingdon, Oxon OX14 4RN

and by Routledge
605 Third Avenue, New York, NY 10158

Routledge is an imprint of the Taylor & Francis Group, an informa business

© 2022 Rose A. Sackeyfio

The right of Rose A. Sackeyfio to be identified as author of this work has been asserted by her in accordance with sections 77 and 78 of the Copyright, Designs and Patents Act 1988.

All rights reserved. No part of this book may be reprinted or reproduced or utilised in any form or by any electronic, mechanical, or other means, now known or hereafter invented, including photocopying and recording, or in any information storage or retrieval system, without permission in writing from the publishers.

Trademark notice: Product or corporate names may be trademarks or registered trademarks, and are used only for identification and explanation without intent to infringe.

British Library Cataloguing-in-Publication Data
A catalogue record for this book is available from the British Library

Library of Congress Cataloging-in-Publication Data
Names: Sackeyfio, Rose A., author.
Title: West African women in the diaspora : narratives of other spaces, other selves / Rose A. Sackeyfio.
Description: Abingdon, Oxon; New York, NY: Routledge, 2022. | Series: African diaspora literary and cultural studies | Includes bibliographical references and index.
Identifiers: LCCN 2021023858 (print) | LCCN 2021023859 (ebook) | ISBN 9781032113067 (hardback) | ISBN 9781032113098 (paperback) | ISBN 9781003219323 (ebook)
Subjects: LCSH: West African fiction (English)–Women authors–History and criticism. | African diaspora in literature. | Women, Black, in literature. | Transnationalism in literature. | LCGFT: Literary critisicm.
Classification: LCC PR9344.S23 2022 (print) | LCC PR9344 (ebook) | DDC 820.9/92870966–dc23
LC record available at https://lccn.loc.gov/2021023858
LC ebook record available at https://lccn.loc.gov/2021023859

ISBN: 978-1-032-11306-7 (hbk)
ISBN: 978-1-032-11309-8 (pbk)
ISBN: 978-1-003-21932-3 (ebk)

DOI: 10.4324/9781003219323

Typeset in Times New Roman
by Newgen Publishing UK

This work is dedicated to my amazing daughters, Naa Borle and Naa Borko, whose love and support inspires my energy and creativity.

I also give thanks to my Ancestors, who remain the architect of every milestone in this earthly abode...

Contents

	Introduction	1
1	Unbelonging, race, and journeys of the self in the diaspora fiction of Buchi Emecheta	13
2	Self and other(s) in *Our Sister Killjoy* by Ama Ata Aidoo	27
3	Violated bodies and displaced identities in Chika Unigwe's *on Black Sisters' Street*	40
4	Negotiating identity and Pan-African aesthetics in *Americanah* by Chimamanda Ngozi Adichie	53
5	Reimagining home(land) and mirrors of the past in *Diplomatic Pounds* by Ama Ata Aidoo	67
6	Unbecoming dreams, splintered identities, and routes of return in Taiye Selasi's *Ghana Must Go*	84
7	Transnational gaze(ing) and shifting identities in the short fiction of Sefi Atta and Chimamanda Ngozi Adichie	98

8 There's no place like home: memory and identity in
  A Bit of Difference by Sefi Atta 111

  Conclusion 124

  Index 131

Introduction

The collection of critical essays in *West African Women in the Diaspora: Narratives of Other Spaces, Other Selves* examines the complexities of transnational identities among African women. Diaspora themes take center stage in ways that reposition women's experiences in African literary expression. This volume reclaims women's voices from the margins of African literary history and project diverse representations of women's experiences in the African diaspora. By foregrounding women's perspectives, the chapters represent the evolution of female-centered writing that has shifted the direction of the African novel in the twenty-first century.

The timeliness of this volume amplifies the production of African women's immigrant writing that began in the mid-1970s with Buchi Emecheta as the forerunner of diaspora fiction. Emecheta's London novels *In the Ditch* (1972), *Second Class Citizen* (1974), *Kehinde* (1994), and *The New Tribe* (2000) represent diaspora perspectives on women's experiences, with the exception of *The New Tribe*, which examines the life of a Nigerian boy in London. Writing in the 1970s, Ama Ata Aidoo crafted *Our Sister Killjoy or Reflections of a Black-Eyed Squint* (1977) so that both women's early narratives lay the groundwork for African women's literature in the global age.

The early narratives of immigrant women's lives push the boundaries away from stereotypical images of women in male-authored works by leading African writers such as Chinua Achebe and Wole Soyinka that span the 1950s and 1970s. Iconic works such as Achebe's groundbreaking *Things Fall Apart* (1955), Soyinka's *The Lion and the Jewel* (1965) and *Death and the Kings Horseman* (1975) are vivid examples as documented by many scholars and critics of African literary history. Since the turn of the century, third-generation women writers have transformed the African literary canon through interrogation of an eclectic array of arresting themes that encompass post-colonial perspectives, feminist

DOI: 10.4324/9781003219323-1

expression, and Afropolitan sentiments. Moreover, local and global tensions and the vagaries of life in diaspora settings, most notably, cultural hybridity are reoccurring tropes in this growing body of works in the twenty-first century. The ways in which migrant women navigate these complexities is the focal point of *West African Women in the Diaspora: Narratives of Other Spaces, Other Selves.*

The global age ushered massive movement of diverse African populations across national borders making transcultural spaces new sites of ethnic, linguistic, and cultural encounters. For African female subjects, shifting identities and disquieting realities transformed notions of *Africanness* and relationships to homeland in myriad and complex ways. Education and opportunities abroad gave migrant women new choices in how to negotiate Western spaces and still maintain African cultural moorings in their lives. The development of African women's immigrant fiction interrogates the transitional and fluid nature of global encounters to create new landscapes of identity for African women. The fictional works in this volume investigate these complicated realities to inspire new trajectories in the African novel. Nana Wilson-Tagoe emphasizes the exploration of the feminine condition in the African novel with the aim to examine how these wider ramifications of women's lives are mapped, "interrogated and reinvented in the medium of the novel. The novel's capacity to map and reorganize reality has made it the most convenient medium for African writers seeking to rethink their social worlds in transitional and postcolonial times" (2009: 177). Fictive narratives by writers from West Africa contribute robust production of successful works that flourish within contemporary settings of social, economic, and political disruption.

In 2004, Ernest Emenyonu, editor of *New Women's Writing in African Literature* (2004: 24) noted the increasing presence of African women onto the literary stage. His editorial, "New Women's Writing, a Phenomenal Rise" lauds the development of women's fiction in the late twentieth century into the global age (Emenyonu 2004: xi–xiii). As one of the leading journals of African literature, a number of volumes published in the twenty-first century are dedicated to the development of women's literary voices on the African continent as well as an important focus on immigrant fiction. Chris Abani (2014) and Mukoma wa Ngugi (2018) have added their voices to celebrate the new trajectories of third generation African women's writing. African women's artistry has come full circle in the twenty-first century to represent a constellation of gendered fictional accounts of self-discovery, relationships to Africa and the interrogation of Western perceptions of the *African self.* The chapters in this volume address a broad range of themes such as hybrid identities, marginalized status, and women's subjectivity beyond Africa's borders.

West Africa claims the spotlight in *West African Women in the Diaspora: Narratives of Other Spaces, Other Selves* to feature writers from Nigeria and Ghana. In Anglophone African literary history, Nigeria features prominently through the pioneering works of early male writers and later female authors of canonical fictional works that define the genre from the colonial era to the post-independence period. Over several decades, Nigerian writers have created a prolific outpouring of fictional works that may be juxtaposed with the preeminence of contemporary works by Nigerian writers in this volume, such as Chimamanda Ngozi Adichie, Sefi Atta, and Chika Unigwe, who carry the legacy of Buchi Emecheta and Flora Nwapa from the early post-independence era into the global age.

Likewise, Ghanaian writers have made their mark in West African literary traditions through significant post-colonial works by Ayi Kwei Armah, Kofi Awoonor, and Nii Ayikwei Parkes among others. Important Ghanaian women writers are Ama Ata Aidoo, Efua Southerland, Ama Darko, and Abena Busia. Notably, successful contemporary writers from Ghana are Taiye Selasi, Yaa Gyasi, and Nana Oforiatta Ayim. In the same way as third-generation writers from Nigeria, diaspora themes command center stage to mirror global mobility of African women as they encounter the intersection of race, class and gender in Western spaces.

Looking closely at literature from West Africa, the region has produced perhaps the largest quantity of writing that increases exponentially in the contemporary age, and writers from Nigeria are disproportionately represented as recipients of literary awards and prizes over the past four decades since Wole Soyinka won the Nobel prize for literature in 1986. Distinguished and iconic writers from other regions of Africa are represented in African literary traditions, but Nigeria's eminency is well noted in the production of post-colonial writing.

The works explored in the volume are unified by theoretical approaches that critically engage post-colonial issues, feminist perspectives, Afropolitan aesthetics, and experiences of diaspora double consciousness or cultural hybridity. Contemporary immigrant literature by African women explicates post-colonial themes as these play out in diaspora sites within a spatio-temporal nexus of global forces of change. New avenues of mobility emerge in an interconnected world when African subjects traverse national, religious, geographical, and linguistic borders. For migrants, diverse locales and intercultural spaces are a dynamic landscape of colliding forces that defies the concept of a 'melting pot'. On the contrary, African identities are unfixed and fluid through exposure to social, economic, and political influences and hybrid cultural spaces of dislocation.

Toward the end of the twentieth century in the groundbreaking work *Modernity, an Introduction to Modern Societies* (1995), Stuart Hall examined fragmented perceptions of the *self* that he called a "crisis of identity for the individual" (597). Hall stated: "The question of 'identity' is being vigorously debated in social theory. In essence, the argument is that the old identities which stabilized the social world for so long are in decline, giving rise to new identities and fragmenting the modern individual as a unified subject" (596). Within a post-modern framework these ideas foreshadow the realities of African migrant women today as expressed in the fiction of third-generation writers who create compelling works of diasporic expression that foreground perceptions of identity. Race, class, and gender mediate and reposition African women's experiences and these evolving realities confound self-definition from African cultural traditions in women's creative works. New diasporic fiction interprets the modalities of geo-spatial and temporal intersections for African subjects. A salient theme infused in contemporary African writing is the prevalence of discomforting experiences of marginalization, otherness, and liminality abroad.

As first-generation authors, the novels of Emecheta and Aidoo represent conventional post-colonial themes that investigate the nation state, neocolonialism, and the problematic behaviors of Africans at home and abroad through the lens of gender. Contemporary writers studied in the book reimagine new forms of post-colonial realities and challenges, paradoxical behaviors, and contradictions that emerge in foreign lands.

A younger generation of African writers engage a range of interrelated post-colonial themes in the novels studied in the volume, such as ineffective leadership in African nations, political corruption, economic crisis, marginalized communities, environmental devastation, and class dynamics among many others. The post-independence landscape poses challenges for women as a driving force to migrate in search of education, employment opportunities and greener pastures in the former colonizing nations as part of the global energies and increased mobility. Post-colonial synergy flows through all the fiction in the volume as a nexus of African immigrant dynamics that reconfigure women's identities. The works that are explored explicate local and global relationships as these determine women's outcomes in Africa, as well as when they journey abroad.

Feminist expression is infused within much of African women's writing to convey women's subjectivity expressed succinctly by Molara Ogundipe Leslie in "The Female Writer and Her Commitment" (1987). Ogundipe-Leslie's articulation has become a tenet of African feminists in the past as well as in twenty-first century fictional expression and is often quoted in the scholarship on African women and feminist theory. Ogundipe-Leslie states: "The female writer has these two major responsibilities; first to tell about being a woman; secondly, to describe reality from a woman's view, a woman's perspective" (5). Though deceptively simple, it speaks to the urgency of African women writing and voicing their truth to the world.

Describing reality in a globalized world is a complex and sometimes contentious process, manifest through a prismatic lens of multiple and competing realities in the African diaspora. Nevertheless, third-generation writers are rising to the challenge by crafting provocative and compelling works as new ways of telling the African story in the global age. The African feminist novel began in 1966 with Flora Nwapa's iconic work, *Efuru*, which usurped unfavorable images of African women in post-colonial works by males. Flora Nwapa is the mother of Anglophone African women's writing, and her pioneering novels recount the lives of Igbo women in Nigeria. Other early feminist works are Mariama Ba's *So Long a Letter* (1989) Ama Ata Aidoo's *Changes* (1991) and Emecheta's three London novels *In The Ditch* (1972), *Second Class Citizen* (1975) and *Kehinde*. (1994) These classic works portray strong female protagonists that critique the customs, traditions, norms, and expectations that shape the lives of African women within indigenous societies. Emecheta's works examine the influence of these modalities in Europe. The portrayal of women characters in these early works paved the way for feminist expression in many subsequent works by African women, and the global age has witnessed an impressive body of woman-centered writing from the diasporic landscape as the central focus of this volume. As the genre continues to evolve, the diversified nature of women's identities inspires the feminist expression of third-generation writers.

Afropolitanism is a concept popularized by Ghanaian-Nigerian writer Taiye Selasi in her well-known and controversial essay, *Bye Bye Babar* (2005). Articulated as a new way of being African in the world, the term has become a trendy, catch phrase in the popular imagination of elite African émigrés whose lives span multi-local spaces, languages and cultures in the cosmopolitan capitals of the world. Framed as a combination of African and cosmopolitan, the term captures the exuberance and celebratory sentiments of educated, mobile and successful Africans in the globalized world of the twenty-first century. According to Selasi:

> Afropolitans belong to no single geography, but feel at home in many ... They (read: we) are Afropolitans-the newest generation of African emigrants, coming soon or collected already at a law firm/chem lab/jazz lounge near you. You'll know us by our funny blend of London fashion, New York jargon, African ethics, and academic successes.

These sentiments are a reflection of Selasi's life as she was born in London as the child of Ghanaian and Nigerian–Scottish parents, having lived in multiple countries, armed with education and mobility. Despite its popularity, Afropolitanism has been criticized, debated, refined, and denied by many writers, scholars, and thinkers who note the reductionist, exclusionary stance infused with privilege and self-congratulatory aesthetics. Essentially, it ignores the masses of African migrants whose dreams of success are smashed against the barriers, restrictions, and resistance of former colonial nations in Europe. The term also ignores the brutal realities of Africans whose lives are marginalized by legal constraints, lack of economic opportunities, and resources to navigate hostile environments that label them as *other.*

Afropolitanism has invigorated robust research and scholarship across disciplines in the humanities and scholars of literature have employed the term as a theoretical lens to interrogate African subjects within diasporic writing. Two important texts are *In Search of the Afropolitan: Encounters, Conversations, and Contemporary Diasporic African Literature* (2016) by Eva Rask Knudsen, and Ulla Rahbek. Another excellent and comprehensive text is Negotiating *Afropolitanism: Essays on Borders and Spaces in Contemporary African Literature and Folklore* (2011) by Jennifer Wawrzinek and J.K.S. Makokha.

Simon Gikandi asserts the merits of Afropolitan:

> To be Afropolitan is to be connected to knowable communities, nations, and traditions; but it is also to live a life divided across cultures, languages, and states. It is to celebrate a state of cultural hybridity – to be of Africa and of other worlds at the same time.
>
> (2010: 9)

Afropolitanism is certainly a useful framework to engage the literature in *West African Women's Writing* through the commonality of women's diaspora perspectives. The ideas that underlie the concept hold the potential to understand women's diaspora experiences. However, the challenge in the use of the term is the avoidance of essentialist analysis because of diversity in education, mobility, and the privilege these factors confer for migrant women and other diaspora subjects. Ato Quayson succinctly places Afropolitanism in context: "The relationship to the homeland is thus not untrammeled by ambiguity, such that what we find in such novels is that the diasporic African is essentially divided between being a true citizen of the world and feeling ambivalent toward the African homeland" (2019: 148).

In looking at the fictional works in *West African Women in the Diaspora*, the aim is to parse out Afropolitan elements as a route to interpreting existential conditions, and the ways in which women renegotiate identities in diverse locales of the African diaspora.

Chapter 1 presents the seminal work of Buchi Emecheta as the godmother of African women's narratives of the diasporic imaginary in London. Post-colonial themes, racialized experiences, and feminist synergy are explored in *Second Class Citizen* (1975 and *In the Ditch* (1974). The novels may be interpreted as women's historical fiction through authentic portrayal of the struggle for self-realization of a Nigerian woman in London. Buchi Emecheta's fictional works have earned a memorable place in the annals of African literary history. Both novels are partly autobiographical and, in addition to post-colonial themes, they represent the complexity of Igbo women's experiences, which is shaped by patriarchy, traditional customs and practices, and feminist/womanist expression that emerge in Europe. The chapter also highlights the ways in which socioeconomic status and class dynamics erect barriers for both African and European women in the London underclass as a subtext of *In the Ditch*. *Second Class Citizen* unfolds the protagonist's life in Nigeria and her transition to an alienating life in London where she must overcome adversity and racial otherness. As a forerunner of African women's writing, Emecheta's contribution is foundational, and her legacy forms a connecting thread to contemporary African women writers, especially those who interrogate race and identity in the African diaspora in the twenty-first century.

Chapter 2 investigates *Our Sister Killjoy* as a postcolonial and feminist classic that illuminates the challenges of Ghanaian immigrants primarily in Germany but also in London. This novel contributes to Emecheta's works that chronicle diaspora journeys for African female migrants. This chapter engages the protagonist's perspectives on the colonial project, neo-colonial realities, and the African experience of hybridity through a gendered lens. Through her insight and sharp critique, the central character responds to a broad range of problems in Europe such as racial difference, the behavior of her fellow Ghanaians, and their refusal to return to Ghana. Postcolonial perspectives are sharply etched in the chapter through examination of hegemonic discourses that frame the colonial encounter in the past. A salient theme addressed in the chapter is the subversion of patriarchy by the female character through her dialogic engagement with male figures. Political consciousness, feminist energies, and the shadow cast over Africa's future lie at the core of the chapter's theme.

Violated Bodies and Displaced Identities in Chika Unigwe's *On Black Sister's Street* is explored in Chapter 3, which describes sex trafficking between Nigeria and Belgium. For women in Nigeria, the post-independence landscape is marred by severe constraints for stability and survival such as economic adversity, moral corruption, and political upheaval as the subject of this chapter. The chapter foregrounds women's vulnerability in patriarchal societies that control women's labor and sexuality in Africa and abroad through the international sex industry. Other factors in Africa that inhibit legitimate means of survival is war and ethnic conflict that may ultimately drive women into the clutches of traffickers. The analysis of the novel unveils the unfortunate outcomes for four women who are enmeshed in local and global forces that motivate the search for success abroad in Belgium. Through the voices of the female characters, the chapter reveals the inner workings of sex trafficking, which include recruitment, objectification, and commodification, and the downward spiral into undocumented status in Europe. The women are essentially sex slaves and the relationship of trafficking to the Atlantic slave trade is highlighted in the chapter.

Chimamanda Ngozi Adichie is Nigeria's, and Africa's, brightest new star in the literary firmament and Chapter 4, "Negotiating Identity and Pan-African Aesthetics in *Americanah*", examines Adichie's explorations of race, identity, and Pan-Africanism through a gendered lens in *Americanah* (2013). The conceptual framework of the chapter articulates an African-centered prism of literary Pan-Africanism expressed by African American scholar, Christel N. Temple in 2006. As an ideology, Pan-Africanism articulates the solidarity, supportive relationships and collaborative interactions of Africans and people of African descent within America as a racially polarizing setting, as well as on the African continent. Written from a diaspora perspective, the novel expounds multi-themed ideas about the construction of racial identity in America along with intra-racial dynamics between the new (recent African immigrants) and old African diaspora formed by the Atlantic slave trade. Adichie's fiction has won critical acclaim, establishing her as the continent's most celebrated contemporary writer. In recent years, Adichie's creative artistry offers critical insights into twenty-first century landscapes of African identity within multi-regional spaces in the global age.

"Reimagining Home(land) and Mirrors of the Past in *Diplomatic Pounds* by Ama Ata Aidoo Ama" is the subject of Chapter 5. Ata Aidoo has broken many years of literary silence with the publication of her third collection of short stories, *Diplomatic Pounds* (2012) whose female characters traverse the boundaries of African women's identity within diaspora spaces of the twenty-first century. Connecting threads of perplexing behaviors bind the stories through the infusion of paradox, discontinuity, and hybrid identities of the female protagonists. A postcolonial framework of analysis accentuates themes of fragmentation, incongruence, and crisis of identity experienced by Ghanaian women immigrants in several of the stories. This chapter will examine these elements in *Diplomatic Pounds* and interrogate the women characters' appropriation of behaviors and ideas that simultaneously alienate them from African cultural norms and familial connections to *home* while offering new spaces to contest their subjectivities in and beyond Africa and its diaspora.

"Unbecoming Dreams, Splintered Identities, and Routes of Return in Taiye Selasi's *Ghana Must Go*" are the issues addressed in Chapter 6. Taiye Selasi's debut novel *Ghana Must Go* (2013) illuminates the complexities of transnational experiences in the African diaspora that spans America, Ghana, and Nigeria. This chapter examines the vividly sketched rendering of multiple perspectives of six family members who are torn between conflicting worlds of difference in the past and the present. The hyphenated lives and splintered dreams of the Sai family wreak emotional havoc, while hybridity and unresolved issues define their reality. The novel highlights the ways in which reconnection to Ghana generates healing from ruptured familial bonds of the past. This chapter will also interrogate the Afropolitan elements of the novel as expressed in transcultural origins and encounters among the Sai family. Scholars and critics of *Ghana Must Go* assert the Afropolitan framing of the work that mirror Selasi's enunciation of the term in the 2005, essay "Bye Bye Babar".

Chapter 7 explores diaspora perspectives of Nigerian women in "Transnational Gaze(ing) and Shifting Identities in the Short Fiction of Sefi Atta and Chimamanda Ngozi Adichie". The short story genre is a fictional landscape to engage the complexities of hybridized existence in the lives of African women émigrés within international settings. This chapter uncovers the layered realities of alienated Nigerian women who navigate *otherness* and marginalization in Western locales in Europe and America. The Nigerian protagonists in Sefi Atta's "A Temporary Position" and in her novella, *News from Home*, experience hyphenated identities in the liminal space of diaspora as racial other(s) in the West.

Similarly, Adichie's "On Monday of Last Week", examines the inner world a lonely woman struggling to survive and to cope with new surroundings. The chapter illustrates the ways in which all the stories unfold the inner journeys of women, the challenges they face as immigrants and the confusing identities they embrace as uprooted subjects in London and America. The central aim of the chapter is to illuminate the contrasting images of Nigeria and the new Western settings of migrant discomfort for the women. "A Temporary Position" contrasts the unproductive economic landscape and bleak outlook in Nigeria with the racial parameters and abrasive nature of life in London. "News from Home" skillfully highlights the effects of severe environmental degradation, and crippling poverty in the Niger Delta of southeastern Nigeria through a feminist lens. Collectively, the stories form a matrix of problems in Nigeria that many observers call a failed state, despite the nation's potential for development through an abundance of natural resources. Seen from abroad, Nigeria's post-colonial challenges place the youth, especially women in difficult circumstances even when they are educated.

"There's No Place Like Home: Memory and Identity in *A Bit of Difference* by Sefi Atta" is the final chapter in the book and chronicles the conflicting experiences of a Nigerian woman who is torn between her country and London, the past and the present, tradition and modernity. As an employee for an NGO, her mobility between multi-local spaces sharpens her gaze on Nigeria in ways that question the value of remaining in London. Contemporary African migration into Western nations has increased steadily over the course of the late twentieth century to a more dramatic exodus from the continent in the global arena. In the search for economic advancement, education and greater opportunities for success, African women grapple with how to reconcile their diaspora perceptions and potential reconnections to home and family. This chapter expands the discourse on local and global tensions in Sefi Atta's 2013 novel, *A Bit of Difference* through analysis of the female protagonist's life in Europe. Her interactions with fellow Nigerians, pressure from her family to marry and return home, and dissatisfaction with her employment fuel her inner conflict. The chapter will trace the protagonist's return to Africa and will illuminate the impact of hybridity on the search for a place called *home*.

The fictional works examined in *West African Women in the Diaspora* unravel the diasporic imaginary as presented by foundational African women writers, alongside the cohort of contemporary authors based in the West. The writers share many concerns for African women as they tackle a broad range of interconnecting issues. The creative artistry of the younger writers reframes post-colonial analysis and feminist sentiments that span the twentieth century into the global era. The volume is unified by the realistic portrayal of inescapable challenges of racial and gender dynamics, as well as the socioeconomic modalities that determine their status in foreign lands. The Western setting of Europe and America becomes a prismatic vista for women to discover new ways of being African in a global world. The diasporic perspective generates nostalgic longing among many African émigrés as a familiar motif in contemporary African literature. The variegated perceptions of female migrants in the fiction are an unstable mixture of contradictions while the search for belonging is ubiquitous in representations of the African diaspora subject.

Works cited

Abani, Chris. *Graceland.* New York. Picador. 2004.
———. *Becoming Abigail.* New York. Akashic. 2006.
Achebe, Chinua. *Things Fall Apart.* London. Heinemann. 1955.
Adichie, Chimamanda Ngozi. *Americanah.* New York. Alfred A. Knopf. 2013.
Aidoo, Ama Ata. *Our Sister Killjoy: Or Reflections of a Black-Eyed Squint.* New York. Longman. 1977.
——— *Changes: A Love Story.* New York. The Feminist Press. 1991.
——— *Diplomatic Pounds & Other Stories.* London. Ayebia Clarke Publishing. 2012.
Ba, Mariama. *So Long a Letter.* London. Heineman. 1989.
Emecheta. Buchi. *In the Ditch.* London. Heineman. 1972.
——— *Second Class Citizen.* London. Allison & Busby.1975.
———. *Kehinde.* London. Heinemann. 1994.
——— *The New Tribe.* London. Heinemann. 2000.
Emenyonu, Ernest. "New Women's Writing: A Phenomenal Rise". *New Women's Writing in African Literature.* Trenton. Africa World Press. 2004. pp. xi–xii.
Gikandi, Simon. "Foreword on Afropolitanism". *Negotiating Afropolitanism: Essays on Borders and Spaces in Contemporary African Literature and Folklore.* Ed. Jennifer Warwrzinek and J.K.S. Makokha. Amsterdam. Rodopi. 2010. pp. 9–11.
Hall, Stuart et al. "A Question of Cultural identity". *Modernity, an Introduction to Modern Societies.* Cambridge. Polity Press. 1995. pp. 595–634.

Knudsen, Eva Rask and Ulla Rahbek. *In Search of the Afropolitan: Encounters, Conversations, and Contemporary Diasporic African Literature*. London. Roman and Littlefield, Ltd. 2016.
Nwapa, Flora. *Efuru*. London. Heinemann. 1966.
———. *Idu*. London. Heinemann. 1970.
———. *Never Again*. Enugu. Trenton. Africa World Press. 1992.
———. *One is Enough*. London. Heinemann. 1992.
Ogundipe-Leslie, Molara. "The Female Writer and Her Commitment". *Women in African Literature Today*. Ed. Eldred Durosimi Jones. London. James Currey. Africa World Press. 1987. pp. 5–13.
Quayson, Ato. "Modern African Literary History: Nation, and Narration, Orality and Diaspora". *Journal of the African Literature Association*. Vol. 13 Issue 1. 2019. pp. 131–150.
Selasi, Taiye. *Ghana Must Go*. New York. The Penguin Press. 2013.
———, "Bye Bye Babar", *LIP*, 3 March 2005.
Soyinka, Wole, *The Lion and The Jewel*. London. Oxford University Press. 1962.
———. *Death and the King's Horseman*. London. Eyre Methuen Ltd. 1975.
Wa Ngugi, Mukoma. *The Rise of the African Novel. Politics of Language, Identity, And Ownership*. Ann Arbor. University of Michigan Press. 2018.
Wawrzinek, Jennifer and J.K.S. Makokha. *Negotiating Afropolitanism: Essays on Borders and Spaces in Contemporary African Literature and Folklore*. Amsterdam-New York. Rodopi. 2011.
Wilson-Tagoe, Nana. "The African Novel and the Feminine Condition". *The Cambridge Companion to the African Novel*. Ed. Abiola Irele. Cambridge. Cambridge University Press. 2009. pp. 177–193.

1 Unbelonging, race, and journeys of the self in the diaspora fiction of Buchi Emecheta

Buchi Emecheta is an important forerunner in the emergence of Anglophone African women's literature and her fiction has earned a memorable place in the annals of African literary history, feminist expression, and post-colonial writing. Emecheta is distinguished as the first African woman to write about the transformative nature of race and gender in the lives of migrant females across national borders of Africa and Europe. This chapter examines the ways in which Emecheta's semi-autobiographical works explore transnational identities of African women in *In the Ditch* (1972) and *Second Class Citizen* (1975). These works are authentic accounts of the complexities and challenges that African women face within discordant Western environments.

Beginning in the twentieth century, global forces in Africa and abroad continue to influence contemporary migratory patterns of African people into cross-cultural spaces of the global north. The transformative nature of new landscapes of opportunity, education, and emerging diaspora identities is the subject of compelling fictional representations by African women authors of whom Emecheta is foundational within this genre. In addition to diaspora themes, Emecheta's oeuvre represents a prolific outpouring of works about African females that are shaped by patriarchy, traditional customs and practices, and feminist/womanist expression. Moreover, *In the Ditch* and *Second Class Citizen* are comparable to the array of contemporary diasporic narratives of leading third-generation African women writers such as Chimamanda Ngozi Adichie, *Americanah* (2013), Sefi Atta's *A Bit of Difference* (2013, Chika Unigwe's *On Black Sisters Street* (2009), NoViolet Bulawayo's, *We Need New Names* (2016), and *Ghana Must Go* (2013) by Taiye Selasie. Other recent fictional works by African women include Yaa Gyasi's sweeping historical novel about Ghana and the diaspora, *Homegoing* (2016). Nana Oforiata Ayim's *The God Child* (2019) and Imbolo Mbue's *Behold the Dreamers* (2016) are also notable

DOI: 10.4324/9781003219323-2

worlds. Bernadine Evaristo was the winner of the 2020 Man Booker Prize for her brilliant short story collection, *Girl, Woman Other* (2020), which unfolds against the European and American diaspora. In 2020 Chika Unigwe published a collection of short fiction, *Better Never than Late* about the Nigerian diaspora in Belgium.

Collectively, this impressive body of works builds upon the literary tradition that began with Emecheta, because the authors engage the mixed bag of African diaspora experiences that (re)shape women's identity. All of the works narrate fictional accounts of the difficulties that arise for women within hybridized spaces of Western nations and their place within global racial hierarchies. In these works, female characters are disaffected, challenged, and marginalized by racial difference along with shifting configurations of African women's status in society. The women protagonists experience adversity and social and racial barriers as a form of initiation into *otherness* as diasporic subjects. Other important themes are sisterhood, relationship to Africa, and coming of age experiences that evokes Fanonian imagery of the divided self that emerges among displaced African subjects. As a literary godmother of African women's fiction, Emecheta's early works convey strong feminist elements that resonate in contemporary women's writing through a matrix of female narratives that connect the past to the present. Further, African immigrant fiction is a dynamic and robust genre that has shifted the direction of African literature away from conventional post-colonial themes that examine issues of the colonial encounter and emerging nationhood to explore new realities of African life in the global age. Contemporary African women's fiction is a richly textured body of works that are crafted in Western environments of contradiction and paradoxical outcomes for many immigrants.

The early 1970s marks the inception of Emecheta's impressive literary corpus, culminating in more than 27 works such as fiction, autobiography, plays, children's books, and young adult fiction. She is widely acknowledged as one of Africa's most well-known writers and is renowned for feminist-inspired works. Emecheta has earned the distinction of being Africa's most prolific female author, and she is known internationally as Africa's foremost feminist. She migrated to London with her husband in 1962 and her major works that were published after *In the Ditch* and *Second Class Citizen* include *The Bride Price* (1976), *The Slave Girl* (1977), *The Joys of Motherhood* (1979), and *Titch the Cat* (1979). During the 1980s she published three children's books: *Nowhere to Play* (1980), *The Moonlight Bride* (1981), and *The Wrestling Match* (1981). The 1980s continued to be her most productive period when she crafted *Destination Biafra* (1982), *Double Yoke* (1982), *Naira Power*

(1982), *Adah's Story* (1983), *The Rape of Shavi* (1983), *Head Above Water* (1984) and *A Kind of Marriage* (1987). *Kehinde* (1994) explores experiences of cultural hybridity against the background of Nigeria and London, similar to her early autobiographical works. Her last novel before her death in 2017 was *The New Tribe* (2000), which unfolds in London, and in this work a Nigerian boy searches for his identity as the adopted son of British parents. African women's identity in Nigeria and abroad lie at the center of Emecheta's enormous contribution to African writing, women's fiction, and feminist-inspired works.

As a literary icon, Buchi Emecheta has been honored with distinguished literary prizes and for *Second Class Citizen* she was awarded the Daughter of Mark Twain award in 1975. She received the Jock Campbell award for *Slave Girl* in 1978 and Best Third World Writer between 1976 and 1979. Most notably, she won the Best Black Writer in Britain award in 1980 for *The Joys of Motherhood*, which is perhaps her crowning achievement in fiction. This novel is widely acknowledged as her most well-known work, has been translated into French and German, and is widely taught.

Buchi Emecheta is the first in a generation of African female writers to highlight the intersection of race, class, and gender in the lives of African women immigrants. Based upon her own life, female characters are at the center of *In the Ditch* and *Second Class Citizen* and, as Nigerian émigrés in London, they experience the harsh realities of alienation, marginalization and the challenge to survive. Emecheta's life and works foreground women's resilience, agency, and pursuit of education while battling adversity, and her success is a testimony of Emecheta's vision of female empowerment. Her literary works express the need for social transformation as women face enormous barriers in life, such as patriarchal oppression, single parenthood, and fewer opportunities for success on the margins of society.

In a well-known interview with Marie Umeh, Emecheta describes herself as a feminist with a small 'f'. According to Umeh:

> Emecheta's literary achievement therefore marks a turning point in Nigerian literary history. For the first time, one observes a conscious effort by a female writer to speak out against the subjugation of Igbo women in the quest for social change.
>
> (1998: 149)

Written from a female perspective, *In the Ditch* and *Second Class Citizen* vividly convey women's subjectivity within the diaspora landscape of London. Adah, the central character, struggles against poverty and marginalization to survive as a single mother of five children. *Second Class Citizen* was written after *In the Ditch* as an examination of the collusion of gender and class dynamics in Nigeria among the Igbo community, and later during her life in London. Emecheta says of her autobiographical work, *Head Above Water* (1986):

> I had to write the book, there was no doubt. I had to reply to those critics who felt that women did not live as I had described in *In the Ditch* and who felt that any woman with a little education should be able to make a living, even though she had a number of children to bring up alone. Writing *Second Class Citizen*, I thought, would give a good background to *In the Ditch*.
>
> (qtd in Sougou 2002: 41)

These sentiments support the ways in which Emecheta's works upholds the commitment of the female writer articulated by Molara Ogundipe-Leslie in *Recreating Ourselves: African Women and Critical Transformations* (1994). More than any other female writer, Emecheta epitomizes her call to African women to tell the woman's story from a woman's perspective (57). Further, Sougou affirms that for Emecheta, "exile spurred her creativity ... and she broaches the issue of migration in her two debut novels, and shows through her characters what it means to be an African and a woman in Britain" (2010: 14). These observations illustrate the synergism of life and art and, through her writing, Emecheta chronicles the gendered realities of African women's singularity.

Moreover, Marie Umeh notes that *Second Class Citizen* describes artistically "how Igbo traditional culture exploits women through a system of assigned and devalued roles that emphasize sexual asymmetry" (1998: 150). Noted for vivid realism, Emecheta unfolds the multilayered forms of subjugation that suppresses the achievements of women in Igbo society. In contrast, Chioma Opara's response is sharply critical of Emecheta's realism and asserts that "Surely, no other West African female writer has written an autobiographical novel as intimate as Emecheta's *Second Class Citizen*. Making the private public in this compelling novel, the author defies traditional norms which frown upon women laying bare their intimate experiences" (2004: 135). Despite such criticism, Emecheta's autobiographical works repositions the female voice in the act of writing back to patriarchy, as well as to interrogate the social, economic, and political forces that hinder female empowerment in society. By inserting herself into history, Emecheta employs writing to reconfigure the African woman's identity in ways that articulate her selfhood as an expression of feminist consciousness.

Carol Boyce Davies sheds light on the power of women's autobiography to expand women's consciousness and to un-silence women from the margins of society. In her article, "Private Selves and Public Spaces: Autobiography and the African Woman Writer", Davies provides a theoretical framework to interpret African women's autobiographical narratives. She formulates three structural modes or levels of narrative self-representation:

1. The self described as synonymous with political struggle
2. The self represented in dialogue with family and/or social cultural history
3. The self identified in resistance to patriarchal/racial order (1991: 278).

These levels represent the modalities of female consciousness in relation to the African woman's world. The Nigerian diaspora space of England infuses the elements of resistance as Emecheta tells her story. *In The Ditch* and *Second Class Citizen* vividly illustrate the ways in which patriarchy, British racism, and class oppression are posed as jointly detrimental to the existence of an African woman in England. But while Igbo scholars have accepted her critique of racism and class oppression, the revealing of unsavory details of female experience under patriarchy has been called "selfish" betrayal (Davies 2013: 287).

Such criticism of Emecheta's honesty and courage highlights the cultural sanctions and conventions of the twentieth century that silenced or muted women's voices within 'traditional' Igbo society. Written in the 1970s, Emecheta's works unfold gender inequality with stark and compelling realism in ways that that posed a challenge to the status quo for women within the conservative climate of the period. In narrating her experiences, Emecheta's pioneering works paved the way for other African women writers and theorists to evolve feminist awareness as a catalyst for social transformation. Nevertheless, *Second Class Citizen* has attained iconoclastic status as a feminist work that is widely acclaimed in the literary world.

In *Second Class Citizen,* Adah begins her story from recollection of her childhood struggles to achieve education that she is denied by her family. This episode in her life recounts the realities of socialization for gender roles within her Igbo community. When her father dies, financial support and preference is given by her relatives to educate her brother and she is forced to use her wits to overcome gender bias. Adah displays strong motivation and determination by earning a scholarship to further her studies. When she completes secondary school, she wants to go further, but realizes that the only route to more education is the stability and security provided by marriage. Thus begins a rocky path to success as the novel reveals a life of subjugation shaped by patriarchy, social constraints for women, and, later on, racial *otherness* in Europe. Adah works at the American embassy in Lagos and supports her husband Francis after he goes to London. This arrangement is essentially a form of exploitation and, two years later, she and her two children join her husband.

In London, Adah experiences racial bias along with many layers of culture shock; perhaps the most vivid of these occurs shortly after her arrival when her husband Francis drives home the reality of racial difference:

> You must know, my dear young lady, that in Lagos you may be a million publicity officers for the Americans; you may be earning a million pounds a day; You may have hundreds of servants: you may be living like an elite, but the day you land in England, you are a second- class citizen. So you can't discriminate against your own people, because we are all second class.
> (Emecheta 1974: 39)

The rude awakening to racial discrimination colors virtually all her experiences as an African woman in London. To illustrate, when she and her husband are searching frantically for housing they are turned away repeatedly and told "Sorry, no colourds" (Emecheta 1974: 70). Adah recalls:

> her house-hunting was made more difficult because she was black; black with two very young children and pregnant with another one. She was beginning to learn that her color was something she was supposed to be ashamed of...She who only a few months previously would have accepted nothing but the best, had by now been conditioned to expect inferior things. She was now learning to suspect anything beautiful and pure. Those things were for the whites, not the blacks.
> (Emecheta 1974: 70)

On one occasion, a woman opened her door to show an apartment to Adah and her husband and "At first Adah thought the woman was about to have an epileptic seizure. As she opened the door, the woman clutched at her throat with one hand, her little mouth opening and closing as if gasping for air..." (Emecheta 1974: 77).

Her predicament is emblematic of the ways in which the confluence of race and gender enmesh her as a 'second class citizen'. Moreover, her deeply troubled marriage is marked by suppression of her identity and self-worth. In this way, the protagonist exposes the effects of racism experienced by Africans in London, which places an undue strain on her marriage, as part of the immigrant experience.

Christine Sizemore aptly notes that Adah carries what Emecheta describes in the title of one of her African novels as a "double yoke": she is expected to be a traditional wife, subservient to her husband, but also to be educated and modern, working to support the family" (1996: 371). Adah and her husband clash repeatedly as his academic pursuits are a downward spiral into failure. He does not work, and retains an iron-like control over Adah, who supports the entire family. Her troubled marriage eventually crumbles under the weight of poor and unwholesome living conditions, inadequate and unsafe childcare, and brutal treatment by her husband.

As an African wife in the grip of patriarchy, Adah has no control over her sexuality and becomes pregnant with a third child. Her feminist consciousness is sparked in response to the unsuitable childcare arrangements that pose a danger to her children. Unable to depend on her husband, she has no choice but to leave her children with an irresponsible white woman whose home is dirty and unsafe. After one of her children becomes ill with viral meningitis, Adah speaks to her husband "in a strange and threatening way...I shall bring Titi home with me and I am not leaving this house to work for you until the kids are admitted into the nursery or you agree to look after them" (Emecheta 1974: 64). These comments signal her resistance against her husband's refusal to assist with childcare. Ada's rebuke of her husband is a temporal marker of her evolving feminist agency to chart her future and provide for her children.

Adah's deteriorating relationship with her husband, arguments, and beatings take their toll and one day, "she did not know where she got her courage from but she was beginning to hit him back, even biting him when need be. If that was the language he wanted, well she would use it" (Emecheta 1974: 154). The idea of a woman fighting back is unthinkable in the context of conventional gender norms and the radical action of the protagonist fuels what Susan Arndt calls *radical feminist writing*. In her insightful book, *The Dynamics of African Feminism: Defining and Classifying African Feminist Literatures* (2002), she frames this type of fiction as works in which "the women characters suffer physical and psychological violence at the hands of men" (85). Other salient characteristics of these works are the absence of any improvement in the woman's circumstances and, in more dramatic developments, the man is killed by the oppressed female, or defeated by the "inability to realize their positive ambitions" (85). This is illustrated by the failure of Adah's husband to complete his studies and develop a successful career in London. Other radical feminist works are Nawal El Saadawi's classic works, *Woman at Point Zero* (1975) and *God Dies by the Nile* (1976) and Chimamanda Ngozi Adichie's bestseller *Purple Hibiscus* (2003). These novels portray dark outcomes because the male oppressor meets a bad end at the hands of a female. Although Emecheta's semi-autobiographical texts do not present violent endings, a woman fighting a man who has abused her physically is nevertheless pivotal and transformative in the life of the protagonist, with strong implications for women's resistance to oppression.

Second Class Citizen and, later, *In the Ditch,* narrate the existence of race, class, and gender as interlocking forms of subjugation for the female protagonist. Susan Arndt affirms that in this body of works, "the suffering of African women characters occurs because of "their socio-economic and/or racial identity. Thus, the gender question is often combined with an examination of other mechanisms of oppression" (2002: 85–86). As the abusive patriarch in the text, Adah's husband reminds her of the layered nature of the barriers she faces in London when he tells her: "You keep forgetting that you are a woman and that you are black. The white man can barely tolerate us men, to say nothing of brainless females like you who could think of nothing except how to breast-feed her baby" (Emecheta 1974: 167). The last straw in the series of unfortunate events is when Francis burns the manuscript of her first book that Adah had pleaded with him to read. The novel ends with her leaving Francis and beginning life afresh as a single parent. Abioseh Porter succinctly notes the

> determined manner in which Adah decides to formally accept responsibility for the children (which had always been hers anyway) are decidedly different from her behavior in most of the earlier scenes... She obviously understands now that she was totally wrong in looking up to Francis as a source of support; she also realizes that if she wants to succeed both in her creative endeavors and in the rearing of her children she has to take full control of her life.
>
> (1996: 271)

These actions represent a total subversion of patriarchy and the development of Adah's inner strength and feminist agency to shape her future.

A new stage in her life as a single parent begins and *In the Ditch* is a metaphor for Pussy Cat Mansions as the setting of the novel. This new environment also represents the ways in which race, class, and gender adversely affect her socioeconomic status as a single parent. Similar to *Second Class Citizen*, the work traces Adah's awakened consciousness of her transcultural identity, strength and determination to educate herself, become a writer and successfully raise her five children alone. Adah narrates that she:

> Knew her problems were going to be many...If the Mansions tenants did not want her, well, she was going to be different. She was not going to be like the other separated mums. At the Mansions, women with kids and no husbands did not go out to work. It was just not done. If you were separated, you lived on the dole. "I am going to be different".
>
> (Emecheta 1972: 21–22)

She works at the Museum but finds it extremely difficult to care for her children effectively. With no options for suitable childcare, she leaves her children in the evening to pursue her studies. Her resolve eventually falters and she quits her job and notes to herself that "joblessness baptized her into Mansions society" (Emecheta 1972: 31). Described in this way, the low-income housing development carries the stigma of dysfunctional and hopeless outcomes for the inhabitants known as 'ditch dwellers'. The title, *In the Ditch*, translates the marginalized space that Adah occupies in the spatial locus of oppression. Her status as diasporic *other* situates her at the bottom, 'in the ditch', while the sides of the ditch represent race and class respectively. Positionality informs her struggle to free herself under seemingly impossible circumstances.

Further, Adah thinks to herself that:

> She, an African woman with five children and no husband, no job, and no future, was just like most of her neighbors-shiftless, rootless, with no rightful claim to anything ... All would stay in the ditch until somebody pulled them out or they sank under.
>
> (Emecheta 1972: 31)

The loss of her job signals an important shift in Adah's transformation as she drops from middle-class to the London underclass as a typical feature of single parenthood. In her new and depressing status among London's 'problem families' Adah is cast to the bottom rung of society, with the expectation of failure and poverty. The system is a form of entrapment but, ironically, it becomes her route to empowerment. She notes the depressing environment because: "the Mansions were a unique place, a separate place individualized for 'problem families'. Problem families with real problems were placed in a problem place. So even if one lived at the Mansions and had no problems the set-up would create problems-in plenty" (Emecheta 1972: 17).

At this point Emecheta introduces an important theme in the novel: survival through sisterhood. Adah's abject poverty, marginalization, and uncertain future fuel her need to join the ditch dweller's association. It is only through her acceptance of and resignation to her plight that she is able to recognize the essential humanity of sisterhood for comfort, security, and camaraderie. Adah's response to oppression and loneliness is manifest through bonding with the female inhabitants of Pussy Cat Mansions. Omar Sougou aptly expresses the idea that: "The novel privileges female space. Women's strength and capacity to resist, to support each other, make up the backbone of the book, from which male dominance is ousted" (2002: 38).

In the London setting, Emecheta has effectively integrated African values of solidarity and sisterhood as a strategy for survival. These events crystalize the feminist themes of the novel through portrayal of women's marginalized status across racial and national boundaries to highlight global gender inequality. The communalistic nature of African society is thus transferred to the London environment in ways that are empowering to all the inhabitants. Marie Umeh observes that *In the Ditch* captures Emecheta's critique of a "system that works to perpetuate broken homes and to foster the growth of dependent, unfilled women on the periphery of an affluent society" (1998: 150). Ada finally inhabits her own space when she moves out of the Pussy Cat Mansions into a more positive environment.

By the end of the novel, she has reconfigured her identity that is forged through sisterhood and struggle. The implications for African womanhood are strength in female bonding, security, and expanded dimensions of empowerment beyond the conventions of marriage. The feminist elements in the novel illustrate that for African women there can be life after marital failure, and beyond poverty and disillusionment. Thus, Emecheta's debut novels confirm the observation by Omar Sougou that "African diaspora subjects articulate identities constructed far away from their homelands or motherlands both in fiction and critical theory" (13). Adah's transformation from victimhood to agency is the core of Emecheta's message of empowered female identity through renegotiating expectations for women in the global arena.

In the Ditch is a chronicle of introspection, maturity and self-confidence that emerges for Adah in the company of women. The novel illuminates the empowering spirit of sisterhood as a strategy for women's survival. This idea resonates in the conceptual framing of feminism, although real world divisions and contradictions emerge through issues of representation, and race and class differences between black and brown women and the white feminist movement in the global north.

In the Ditch illustrates that women's collective engagement may be harnessed for empowerment when barriers of socioeconomic status are leveled, as portrayed in the novel. All of the women in the 'Mansions' are single, poor, and struggling as dependents of the state. The development of awakened feminist consciousness while battling adversity resonates Katherine Franks's framing in "Women Without Men: The Feminist Novel in Africa". With reference to energies of social transformation, she observes that:

> Given the historically established and culturally sanctioned sexism of African society, there is no possibility of a compromise, or even truce with the enemy. Instead, women must spurn patriarchy in all its guises and create a safe, sane, supportive world of women: a world of mothers and daughters, sisters and friends.
>
> (1987: 15)

The work portrays the feminist commitment to reconfigure marginalized identities for African women in England. The novel's ending unravels the ways in which Adah's character has come full circle as a self-actualized woman in control of her sexuality, and her destiny. The transnational space of London situates the heroine in a hostile environment that erodes her dignity through barriers of otherness, gender oppression, and poverty. Both novels form a portrait of female resilience in the midst of adversity and Emecheta's fiction is a celebration of women's capacity for strength, endurance, and creative expression.

In the Ditch and *Second Class Citizen* project emerging feminist consciousness that drives the protagonist towards self-actualization. The ability to survive all odds as a black woman and single parent of five children in London vividly captures the spirit of women's potential to survive without a husband. Emecheta's literary works express the need for social transformation as women face multilayered and complex obstacles to upward mobility and success in life.

Second Class Citizen and *In the Ditch* foreground African women's experiences, self-determination, and potential for transformation in society. Both works illustrate the development of personhood in the midst of *otherness* and uncertainty in Europe. Emecheta's contribution to changing the image and representation of African women in life and literature follows the tradition of her generation, which includes Flora Nwapa, Mariama Ba, and Ama Ata Aidoo as early African women writers who wrote women's truth within a post-colonial, feminist literary tradition. In *Second Class Citizen* and *In the Ditch,* Emecheta passionately conveys the brand of unrelenting patriarchy that smothers women's identity, silences their voices, and crushes their dreams. She effectively displays how these forces are usurped through a woman's resistance and sheer determination to succeed. The mandate for women's education as a route to empowerment is the strongest measure to displace patriarchal structures of dependency and oppression.

Despite the binding nature of social, economic, and racial barriers, Emecheta reimagines what it means to be an African woman at home and in the diasporic landscape of Europe.

Emecheta's novels are compelling narratives because of the authentic and vivid rendering of the lived realities of an African woman. *Second Class Citizen,* and *In the Ditch* are groundbreaking and pioneering works that inspired the production of robust, authentic women's writing in the global age of mobility, transformation, and flux.

Works cited

Adichie, Chimamanda Ngozi. *Purple Hibiscus.* Lagos. Farafina. 2003.
——— *The Thing Around Your Neck.* Toronto. Alfred A. Knopf. 2009.
——— *Americanah.* Toronto. Alfred A. Knopf. 2013.
Aidoo, Ama Ata. *Our Sister Killjoy: Or Reflections of a Black-Eyed Squint.* Lagos/New York. Nok Press. 1979.
Arndt, Susan. *The Dynamics of African Feminism: Defining and Classifying African-Feminist Literatures.* Translated by Isabel Cole. Trenton. Africa World Press. 2002.
Atta, Sefi. *News from Home.* Northampton. Interlink Books. 2010.
——— *A Bit of Difference.* Northampton. Interlink Books. 2013.
Ayim, Nana Oforiatta. *The God Child.* London. Bloomsbury. 2019.
Bulawayo, NoViolet. *We Need New Names.* New York. Regan Arthur Books. 2013.

Davies, Carol Boyce. "Private Selves and Public Spaces: Autobiography and the African Woman Writer". *College Language Association Journal.* Vol. XXXIV. No. 3. 1991. pp. 267–289.

Emecheta, Buchi. *In the Ditch.* London. Heineman. 1972.

——— *Second Class Citizen.* London. Allison & Busby. 1975.

——— *The Bride Price,* London. Allison & Busby; New York: George Braziller. 1976.

——— *The Joys of Motherhood.* New York. George Braziller.1979.

——— *Titch the Cat.* London. Allison & Busby. 1979a.

——— *Nowhere to Play.* London. Allison & Busby. 1979b.

——— *The Moonlight Bride.* London: Oxford University Press. 1980a.

——— *The Wrestling Match.* London: Oxford University Press. 1980b.

——— *Naira Power.* London. Macmillan. 1982a.

——— *Double Yoke.* London. Ogwugwu Afor Co. Ltd. 1982b.

——— *Destination Biafra.* London. Allison & Busby. 1982c.

——— *The Rape of Shavi.* London. Oguwu Afor. 1983.

——— *A Kind of Marriage.* London. Macmillan. 1986a.

——— *Head Above Water.* London. Fontara. 1986b.

——— *Kehinde.* London. Heinemann. 1994.

——— *The Slave Girl.* New York. George Braziller. 1997.

——— *The New Tribe.* London. Heinemann. 2000.

Evaristo, Bernadine. *Girl, Woman, Other.* New York. Grove Press. 2019.

Fanon, Franz. *Black Skin, White Masks.* Trans. Charles Lam Markmann. New York.

Frank, Katherine. "Women Without Men: The Feminist Novel in Africa". *Women in African Literature Today.* 15. Trenton. Africa World Press. James Currey. 1987. pp. 14–34.

Mbue, Imbolo. *Behold the Dreamers.* New York. Penguin Random House. 2016.

Ogundipe-Leslie, Molara. *Recreating Ourselves: African Women and Critical Transformations.* Trenton, Africa World Press. 1994. pp. 57–67.

Opara, Chioma. *Her Mother's Daughter: The African Writer as Woman.* Port Harcourt. University of Port Harcourt Press. 2004. pp. 131–142.

Porter, Abioseh Michael. "*Second Class Citizen.* The Point of Departure for Understanding Buchi Emecheta's Major Fiction". *Emerging Perspectives on Buchi Emecheta.* Ed. Marie Umeh. Trenton, Africa World Press. 1996. pp. 267–275.

Saadawi, Nawal El. *Woman at Point Zero.* London. Zed Books. 1975.

——— *God Dies by the Nile.* London. Zed Books. 1976.

Sackeyfio, A. Rose. "Frames of Marginality: Emecheta's Legacy in the 21st Century". *Praxis Journal of Gender and Cultural Studies.* Vol. 26. No. 1/2 Spring/Fall. 2018. pp. 21–34.

Sizemore, Christine. "The London Novels of Buchi Emecheta". *Emerging Perspectives on Buchi Emecheta.* Ed. Marie Umeh. Trenton. Africa World Press. 1996. pp. 367–385.

Sougou, Omar. *Writing Across Cultures: Gender, Politics and Difference in the Works of Buchi Emecheta*. Amsterdam-New York. Rodopi. 2002. pp. 29–55.

―――― "Ambivalent Inscriptions: Women, Youth and Diasporic Identity in Buchi Emecheta's Later Fiction". *African Literature Today*. Vol. 27. Ed. Ernest Emenyonu. London. James Curry. 2010. pp. 13–27.

Umeh, Marie. "Buchi Emecheta". *Postcolonial African Writers: A Bio-Bibliographical Critical Sourcebook.* Ed. Pushpa Naidu Parekh and Siga Fatima Jagne. London. Routledge. 1998. pp. 148–163.

Unigwe, Chika. *Better Never than Late*. Abuja-London. Cassava Republic. 2020.

2 Self and other(s) in *Our Sister Killjoy* by Ama Ata Aidoo

Aidoo's classic, *Our Sister Killjoy* (1977) engages post-colonial and feminist discourse in ways that foreground an African woman's experience in the Ghanaian diaspora. The term "Black-eyed Squint" is a metaphorical signifier of her gaze, that captures the spatio-temporal nexus of Ghana and Africa's encounter with the West. Sissie, the female protagonist becomes acutely aware of her *blackness* primarily in Germany and later in London. Sissie's coming of age to racialized perceptions of Africans by Europeans is measured against her ethnic identity, cultural integrity, and the ravages of colonization in her country. This chapter argues that her 'squint' is actually the clear-sighted vision of a former colonial subject whose eyes are open to the unseemly transformations and legacy of the colonial past. From her vantage point as a transnational subject, Sissie interrogates the colonial project, the mental impact on her fellow Africans, and the confluence of gendered expectations at home and abroad.

Ama Ata Aidoo is internationally acclaimed and garners distinction as the first African woman to write a play in English with the publication of her signature work *The Dilemma of a Ghost* (1965) and later *Anowa* (1970). Her first collection of short stories is *No Sweetness Here* (1970), followed by her diaspora novel *Our Sister Killjoy: Or Reflections of a Black-Eyed Squint* (1977) and a volume of poetry, *Someone Talking to Sometime* (1985). Her children's book, *The Eagle and the Chickens and Other Stories* was published in the same year. In 1987 she penned a second collection of poetry called *Birds and Other Poems*, and a third, volume, *An Angry Letter in January* (1992). *Changes, a Love Story* (1991) is a widely celebrated novel that won the Commonwealth Prize in 1992. Her latter works are collections of short stories, *The Girl Who Can and Other Stories* (1997) and *Diplomatic Pounds & Other Stories* (2012) and a collection of poetry, *After the Ceremonies* in 2017.

DOI: 10.4324/9781003219323-3

As one of the godmothers of Anglophone African women's fiction, her works command a special place in the canon of post-colonial writing that spans the twentieth and twenty-first centuries. As an iconic female author, Ama Ata Aidoo stands alongside Buchi Emecheta through interrogation of women's identities in West Africa and the borderlands of Europe as expressed through their early works. Both women paved the way for the contemporary generation of writers to elaborate the gendered experiences of women in the geo-spatial loci of the West. *Our Sister Killjoy* is also an odyssey into racialized identity and post-colonial subjectivity, but the female protagonist awakens to a new consciousness of her place in the world on her own terms.

Further, Ghanaian women authors in the global age are building upon her legacy through connecting threads of diaspora fiction that chronicle similar experiences of African immigrant women. Contemporary Ghanaian literature like Taiye Selasi's highly acclaimed *Ghana Must Go* (2013), Yaa Gyasi's epic novel *Homegoing* (2016) and her recent work *Trancendent Kingdom* (2020) represent the trajectory of female-authored works that expand the genre of Ghanaian immigrant women's fiction. Another recent work by a Ghanaian writer is Nana Oforiatta Ayim's debut novel *The God Child* (2019), which vividly frames the Ghanaian–German identities of women living in the margins of diaspora confusion. This body of emergent fictional works forms a tapestry of literary history that foregrounds the dynamics of hybridity as a prominent theme.

Aidoo is an avowed feminist writer whose literary corpus spans the genres of fiction, drama, and poetry and her works have been interpreted as 'writing back' to patriarchy, colonization, neo-colonialism, and the attendant 'colonial mentality' among her fellow Africans. Similar to Buchi Emecheta's London novels, *In the Ditch* (1972) and *Second Class Citizen* (1974), Aidoo interrogates women's role and status in African society as well as in the diaspora locales of Europe. In *Our Sister Killjoy,* Aidoo draws upon her own experiences in London and Germany. One of the most important features of the work is the centrality of the female voice that conveys cross-cultural perspectives of Africans in relation to Europeans. Angeletta Gourdine notes that "Sissie reflects that London, or England could never be her colonial home. Her entire journey highlights the ways in which colonialism has cannibalized the history of her homeland" (2002: 95).

The novel is structured in four sections that mark the protagonists' journey into *otherness* in Europe. Sissie's visit begins when she enters "Into a Bad Dream" that foreshadows the dark undertones of racialized identity and post-colonial gaze(ing) of the protagonist as a cultural outsider through the lens of her female subjectivity.

Sissie's reflections are expressed through a third-person narrator as well as the poetic interjections of other speakers in the work. Before departing Ghana, her gaze looks northward and she reflects: "It is a long way from home to Europe. A cruel past, a funny present, a major desert or two, a sea, an ocean, several different languages apart, airplanes bridge the skies" (Aidoo 1977: 8). The all-encompassing and panoramic vista spans historical and hegemonic relationships, as well as the geographical and linguistic divide of the 'global north' and African nations. Her gaze shifts from the past to the present and ultimately the future. These images evoke Sissie's position as a postcolonial subject and her agency to voice the legacies of social, economic, and political disruptions within her formerly colonized nation. With reference to Aidoo's literary corpus, Vincent Odamtten asserts that "we may see her work as progressing toward an increasingly complex vision of Ghanaian society and global politics" (1994: 13). Ghana became independent from Britain in 1957, and Aidoo's observations are vivid and authentic recollections of the post-independence landscape of Ghanaian immigrants.

Haiping Yang emphasizes that *Our Sister Killjoy* is "one of the most prominent texts of twentieth century world literatures" (1999: 94). Further, he notes that Sissie's identity as a transnational subject affirms the "fluid formations of 'in-between hybrids' and their critiques, one may argue, indicate the high significance of the tropes of "borderland subjectivity" (1999: 93). Moreover, Gay Wilentz in "The Politics of Exile: Reflections of a Black-Eyed Squint in *Our Sister Killjoy*" underscores the ways in which the "novel exposes a rarely heard viewpoint in literature in English – that of the African woman exile; Aidoo's protagonist Sissie, as the 'eye' of her people, is a sojourner in the 'civilized' world of the colonizers" (1999: 79). In this way, Sissie shifts the transcontinental gaze to a woman-centered account of her experiences and, shortly after her arrival in Germany, she enters into "a Bad Dream" as an African woman.

Sissie is a student who is offered a scholarship to attend a workshop in Germany and a visit to England. Her first encounter with covert racism occurs on the flight to Germany, when she is asked to move to the rear of the plane to join fellow African passengers. Racial hierarchies haunt the work through Aidoo's skillful use of imagery, which discloses the stark differences between Africa and Europe, revealed during her overnight flight from Ghana to Germany. Soon after take-off Sissie observes that the flight passes over Africa in "the dead of night" (1977:

10). "So that it was nearly dawn when they crossed the Mediterranean Sea. And as they left Africa there was this other continent, lighted up with the first streaks of glorious summer sunshine" (11). Aidoo invokes European colonial representations of Africa in ways that conjure Joseph Conrad's infamous novella, *Heart of Darkness* (1889), which captures the colonial representation of Africa as the dark continent. Sissie's voyage unravels a 'squinted gaze' at the distorted binaries of light and dark that juxtapose perceptions of civilized Europe and primitive Africa. When she thinks "Good night Africa. Good Morning Europe" (1977: 11) it suggests the dawn of civilization in relation to herself as "a lowland born" (11). Throughout the work, Aidoo, speaking through Sissie, sarcastically presents the European perception of herself as the abject and contemptible African *other*.

In Germany while strolling around the city:

> Suddenly, she realized a woman was telling a young girl who must have been her daughter: 'Ja das Schwattze Madchen'. From the little German that she had been advised to study for the trip, she knew that 'das Schwattze Madchen' meant 'Black girl'? ... And it hit her. That all that crowd of people going and coming in all sorts of directions had the color of the pickled pig parts that used to come from foreign places to the markets at home.
>
> (Aidoo 1977: 12)

Sissie's jarring awareness of racial otherness heightens her culture shock and the abrasive experience sharpens her gaze, not only outward, but inward to feelings of regret that, for the rest of her life, she will harbor her recollection of "the moment when she was made to notice difference in human colouring" (1977: 13). Moreover, recent works by contemporary African women writers mirror the impact of racial difference in the experiences of African women that travel abroad. Chimamanda Ngozie Adiche's bestseller *Americanah* (2013) and Sefi Atta's *A Bit of Difference* (2013) depict disquieting realities of *blackness* in Western spaces through a gendered lens.

Aidoo positions her protagonist to parallel her own discomfort with racial otherness in contrast to systematic forms of domination in the European colonizing mission in Africa. In poignant sentiment, Sissie notes that "what she also came to know was that someone somewhere would always see in any kind of difference, an excuse to be mean" (Aidoo 1977: 13). Despite her shame at her own prejudice and repulsion to Germans, her critical stance highlights the brutal exploitation, plundering and rape of "land, land, and more land ... and resources like

Gold and silver mines, Oil, Uranium, Plutonium ... and inevitably, all consuming 'Power to decide who is to live, who is to die'" (13). She sadly recounts the erosion of African cultures and, in the case of Ghana, assimilation of the English language. The text moves fluidly to poetic narrative to recollect the European plundering of: "Our tongue / Our Life- while our / Dead fingers clutch / English" (28–29).

Aidoo subverts the victimhood trope as Sissie is un-silenced by speaking back to the purveyors of colonial intrusion. These musings presage the nature of Sissie's discomforting sojourn in a space of marginality. The specter of death infuses the dark undertones of the work, suggesting that post-colonial Ghanaians are mere shadows of their former (African) selves as they embrace the trappings of Western life. When contemplating her youthful peers, Sissie notes that, unlike foreign aid workers and volunteers from the West who participate in development projects in Africa, the labor of her companions is not needed in Germany. She describes them as mainly "laughing, singing, sleeping and eating" (Aidoo 1977: 35). These uneven realities form the context of less-developed nations and Western structures of aid. Sissie's incriminating stance chides African and other "Third World ... Rulers Asleep to all things at All times-Conscious only of Riches, which they gather in a Coma" (34). Her observation of neo-colonial power structures among Africa's elite is integral to the work's engagement with post-independence entropy.

She knows her companions will never question the political implications of their adventure in Europe and suggests that they are secure in the knowledge of what they will become in the future: "Diplomats, Visiting Professors, Local experts in sensitive areas Or Some such hustlers" (Aidoo 1977: 35). These ideas represent Aidoo's perspectives on African neo-colonial elite who inherit unmerited and questionable spaces of privilege in the post-colonial landscape. In calling them 'hustlers' she forecasts the dubious roles they will play in the process of nation-building and development. This does not bode well for post-independence Africa, still reeling from the onslaught of foreign jurisdiction. Essentially, she and the other students do no work and because of their 'difference' are essentially objects of curiosity to their German hosts.

Sissie's odyssey in Germany continues in the section called "Plums" that frames a bewildering relationship with a woman named Marija. The friendship unfolds through disjointed, uneven exchanges that sharply contrast their differences in personal characteristics and cultural background against the backdrop of European hegemonic formalities. The protagonists' dilemma in Germany heightens the ways in which space determines social relations and racial dynamics. The response to Sissie's *blackness* is primarily described through her friendship with Marija. In public spaces, she stands out more because of her gender, and the exotic nature of her appearance that attracts unwarranted attention. Sissie recounts the "way they gaped at her, pointing at her smile. Her nose. Her lips. Their own eyes shining. Not expecting her to feel embarrassed" (Aidoo 1977: 43). In one encounter, an old man begins pointing first to his arm then to Sissie's arm in apparent disbelief at the difference in skin color. Despite being puzzled, Sissie is comfortable in her own skin, even when Marija offers no explanation.

Unknown to Sissie, she is being courted by Marija and the developing friendship is actually an inverted form of seduction. Sissie is showered with gifts of food and an overabundance of fruit, especially plums. The idea of 'strange fruit' heightens the metaphorical dimensions of the work, because Sissie acknowledges that the succulent plums: "owed their glory ... to other qualities that she herself possessed at that material time: Youthfulness / Peace of Mind/Feeling free: / Knowing you are a rare article / Being Loved" (Aidoo 1977: 40). Further, Sissie "ate the plums, caressing the plump berries with skin color almost like her own" (95). The imagery is sensual and erotic, suggesting the attraction of the two women and Sissie is clearly fascinated by the plums that she has never seen before.

Aidoo is noted for economy of words in her writing that is vividly apparent in symbolic elements that envision Sissie as the object of Marija's attention. Sissie's characterization of herself is a form of self-affirmation, although to Marija she is the exotic black *other* and available for a relationship. Aidoo cleverly parallels the representation of Sissie's corporeality as succulent and desirable to the wanton pursuit of Africa's wealth by Europeans. These ideas form a subtext of the relationship between the two women as well as Marija's absent husband as representation of Germany's militaristic past, colonizing ventures, and genocidal assault against the Jews. Her husband, who never appears, is called "Big Adolph" and her infant son is "little Adolph". Marija's overtures towards Sissie come to a head when, in Marija's bedroom, she:

> felt Marija's cold fingers on her breast. The fingers of Marija's hand touched the skin of Sissie's breasts while her other hand groped round and round Sissie's midriff, searching for something to hold on to. It was the left hand that woke her up to the reality of Marija's embrace. The warmth of her tears on her neck. The hotness of her lips against hers. As one does from a bad dream, impulsively Sissie shook herself free. With too much effort, unnecessarily, so that she

unintentionally hit Marija on the right cheek with the back of her right hand.

(1977: 64)

Susan Arndt states that: "When Marija's lips touch her, Sissie breaks free-escaping both the seizing of her body and the history of *white* appropriation of black bodies" (2012: 121).

Sissie's reactions are a mixture of sorrow and the wish that she was male.

Sissie notes the acute loneliness that surface when a "young Aryan housewife kisses a young black woman with such desperation" (Aidoo 1977: 64). Shortly after this incident, when Sissie tells Marija she is leaving, tense conversations unfold between them. The thought of Sissie abruptly leaving Germany is awkward and painful for Marija and, in a kind of twisted irony, Sissie admits "that there is pleasure in hurting. A strong three-dimensional pleasure, an exclusive masculine delight that is exhilarating beyond all measure" (76).

Further, Sissie is the embodiment of a 'killjoy' in the compassionless exit from a meaningless liaison and her regret at causing pain is at best superficial. Aidoo conveys feminist energies by positioning Sissie's response to resonate masculinity that will assert her voice, and her agency in the gender dynamics of her friendship with Marija. This is questionable because it is insensitive, even as Sissie assumes a masculine stance to claim her autonomy. Hildegarde Hoeller also notes that: "Sissie slips into a male narrative, one of violence and cruelty against the other, with an almost imperial disregard for the humanity of the other" (2004: 139). This interpretation is exaggerated because there is no physical act of violence in this regard; however, Sissie's actions represent resistance to Marija as retribution for the brutality of Europeans against Africans.

This turn of events suggests that Adioo transposes hegemonic discourses and legacies of power relationships between Africans and Europeans. Sissie's inverted gaze disrupts the 'victimhood trope' of Africa's engagement with foreign intruders as well as to reassert African agency through shifting perspectives of the protagonist. As a symbolic gesture, Sissie's rejection of Marija's advances signal the possibilities for reclamation of the African 'self' from European entanglement in the post-colonial era. Her abrasive physical response is reflexive, asserted with abruptness that stuns the narrative structure. She recalls that she awakens "as one does from a bad dream, impulsively" (Aidoo 1977: 64). Thus, Sissie's 'squint' conveys the impossibility of complicity in her own entrapment. The seductive nature of Marija's actions, coupled with

Sissie's rejection, is a post-colonial allegory of Africa's redemptive power through an awakened consciousness as post-independence subjects.

The section called "From Our Sister Killjoy" chronicles Sissie's experiences in England, the site of Ghana's former colonial authority. Her 'black-eyed squint' examines her fellow Africans and her perceptions are lucid, honest, and caustic. Among other contradictions, Sissie is surprised at the number of black immigrants that mirror the vestiges of the former colonial relationship of Britain to Ghana. She notes that: "The place seemed full of them but they appeared to be so wretched, she wondered why they stayed …. Sissie bled as she tried to take the scene in" (Aidoo 1977: 85).

Sissie's observations are much like those of a skilled photographer, who, in capturing an image, adjusts the lens to create a nuanced portrait of the subject. One of the most hurtful realizations for her is the shabby, wretched appearance of badly-dressed Africans, especially the women whom she describes as "pitiful" (88).

In her anger, she cannot understand why Africans remain abroad under such deplorable conditions as well as the refusal to tell the truth about Europe when they visit home as "been-to's" (91). She imagines the "women who at home would have been dignified matrons" (88). In this way, Sissie's positionality informs her views in ways that unhinge her naïve expectations about post-independence progress. The intensity of her reaction is magnified given the context of the colonial past, and the vagaries of the neo-colonial landscape that is riddled with unearned privilege, dubitable behaviors, and counter-productive forms of development. The longer she is in London, the more critical she becomes while her 'squint' casts a critical eye on the deportment of her fellow Africans. Her anger is penetrating as she observes that "against any other skin, such an assemblage of rags would have made the people look even more ridiculously pathetic than those Africans and West Indians actually did" and notes that "in a cold land, poverty shows as nowhere else" (88). The abject immigrant experience confirm that she has indeed entered into a "bad dream" in Europe.

As her awareness deepens, she takes in the full range of migrants, many of whom are perpetual students who never complete their studies. She describes them as "recipients of the leftovers of imperial handouts" (Aidoo 1977: 87). Essentially, she calls out the bourgeois class as sell-outs who act in service of their former colonial masters in ways that subvert the interests of their people in Africa. Sissie recalls that the "story is as old as empires. Oppressed multitudes from the provinces rush to the imperial seat because that is where they know all salvation comes from" (87). The irony is that, in the past, such populations eventually discover that "for the slave, there is nothing at the center but worst slavery" (88). Sissie's indictment articulates the well-known syndrome of 'colonial mentality'. Her transcontinental gaze informs her views in ways that cut through naïve assumptions about post-independence progress.

The final section of the novel is written in the form of a love letter that is actually a polemical discourse expressed in strong feminist narrative. Written during the final stages of her journey home, the letter expresses a conflation of the salient themes in the text: post-colonial and neo-colonial reckoning, and feminist synergy. In "The Feminist Impulse and Social Realism in Ama Ata Aidoo's *No Sweetness Here* and *Our Sister Killjoy*", Chimalum Nwankwo succinctly corroborates these intersections when he notes that the novel illustrates that:

> the problems of the African woman are expressed as integral parts of the problems of colonial and postcolonial Africa. Aidoo's feminist concerns are not treated in isolation from Africa's political instability, the new master complex of the so-called elite, the atavistic problems of the rural African at the cross-roads of history, the fury and impotence of the radical African, the lure of the Western world and so forth.
>
> (1986: 152)

Moreover, Sackeyfio emphasizes that "Postcolonial realities form the historical, political and economic context of the status and roles of African women" (2007: 74). She notes that another of Aidoo's novels, *Changes*, also examines the impact of the post-independence landscape through imposition of Christianity, Victorian values, patriarchy, and capitalism (74).

Feminist energies dominate the text that translates to speaking back to gendered expectations, and the articulation of women's agency, as well as Sissie's female voice that intrudes into male-centered spaces of political debate. Sissie's narrative voice is authoritative and robust through discursive engagement with unresolved issues of social, economic, and political outcomes for Africa. The letter is crafted as a dialogue of sorts between Sissie and the man she not only rejects but leaves behind in London to return to Ghana. Apart from addressing her spurned lover, she also challenges the ideas of her African brothers in Europe for their corrupted values and lack of commitment to their homeland. In an interview, Aidoo confirms that: "Sissie uses her boyfriend, her ex-boyfriend actually, as the conduit through which she is speaking with a communal voice, a kind of collective voice" (Needham 1995: 129).

Thus, Sissie's reflections represent a collective 'oppositional' gaze on the multilayered complexities of Africans who travel to Europe. The tone of the letter is a mixture of sarcasm, sharp rejoinders to questions raised, and reasoned logic to contextualize the challenging circumstances that Africans have faced in their encounters with Europe.

Sissie's feminist voice is honest in the admission that she is in love, although in no uncertain terms. She writes: "That desiring you as I do, needing you as I do, I still let you go" (Aidoo 1977: 117). She boldly rejects the conventional behaviors of dependent women who pursue men at all costs:

> They say that any female in my position would have thrown away everything to be with you, and remain with you: first her opinions, and then her own plans. But oh deliciously naïve me. What did I rather do but daily and loudly criticize you and your friends for wanting to stay forever in alien places.
>
> (117)

She is also told that since she knew where he lived she should simply apologize and basically "Cream up to him ... If you love your man, take him by any means necessary" (119).

Moreover, Sissie provides a historical context of gendered behaviors that privilege males in ways that undermine female autonomy. She notes that societal expectations of passive behavior for women are the result of "Some kind of hashed up Victorian notions" (117).

Aidoo articulates the belief that European colonization influenced behaviors and norms for African women that eroded sociocultural, economic, and political roles within indigenous societies. Colonization established rigid patriarchal structures in Africa through Christianity and Victorian values that privileged males and relegated women to subordinate status in the domestic realm and in the larger society.

Sissie's voice takes the lead to affirm her displeasure with Africans who flock to Europe and remain there. Aidoo inserts a broader context of European predatory engagement with Africa that begins with slavery. She refers to scientific racism as "pseudo-scientific junk" (Aidoo 1977: 114) to justify the European need for free labor and utters a "curse on those who for money would ruin the Earth and trade in human miseries" (115). She utters "A curse on all those who steal continents" (120). These ideas are scathing, but Sissie diverts her critique to her countrymen and admits to losing sleep over why they remain abroad after completing their studies. This is incomprehensible to her since the post-colonial agenda was to utilize the knowledge acquired abroad to achieving nationhood back home.

In a vivid flashback, Sissie recollects a meeting of the students' union where she angrily "attacks everybody" (Aidoo 1977: 121) with questions about their misplaced loyalties, shallow thinking, and pathetic excuses. The reasons given are lack of employment opportunities, inadequate remuneration commensurate with their skills, the need to build homes for their long-suffering African mothers, and other superfluous reasons. Finally, in frustration, she resigns herself to the futility of the situation and knows that she will never mail the letter. As her flight nears Ghana, she welcomes the cathartic release of her pain and decides to "let things lie where they have fallen" (133). Sadly, she envisions future returnees to Africa who will become "ghosts of the humans that they used to be" (89).

Finally, Sissie's brief sojourn in Europe is an exploration of post-colonial 'gazing' through the gendered lens of a Ghanaian female student. Kathryn Frank aptly interprets the idea that Sissie is "an African Everywoman, and the novel charts her solitary odyssey towards freedom. 'Killjoy' underlines her essential isolation" (1987: 29).

The novel's heroine is a woman whose vision of the past forms an elliptical arc of discontinuity and unresolved issues in Africa's future. Sadly, the disruptive legacies of the colonial encounter resonate unsettling realities through gendered borderland experiences as the dominant narrative in *Our Sister Killjoy*. In sum, the vivid portrayal of the experiences of a young Ghanaian woman in Germany is episodic, as a short visit to Europe where she enters a space of racial 'difference'.

During her sojourn in Germany, she becomes a racial *other* but is never unmoored of her cultural authenticity, female identity, or political consciousness. The geographical space of Europe affords a vantage point for Sissie to reassess and to reenvision her place in the paradoxical landscape of post-independence. In remaining true to herself, strong feminist ideas and behaviors inform her choice to reject unsuitable partners whether female or male and the strength to speak truth to the African men she encounters. In *Our Sister Killjoy,* Aidoo underscores the centrality of women to deconstruct the complexities of European domination and oppression with implications for women and men, as well as for African nations in flux. Sissie's perceptions drive home the idea that colonization damaged Africa beyond the social, economic, and political upheaval. The novel unfolds the ways in which former colonial subjects are sometimes their own worst enemies.

Works cited

Adichie, Chimamanda Ngozi. *Americanah*. Toronto. Alfred A. Knopf. 2013.
Aidoo, Ama Ata. *No Sweetness Here*. New York. The Feminist Press. 1970.
―― *Anowa*. New York. Longman. 1970.

―――― *The Dilemma of a Ghost and Anowa*. Essex. Longman. 1965.
―――― *Our Sister Killjoy: Or Reflections of a Black-Eyed Squint.* New York. Longman. 1977.
―――― *Someone Talking to Sometime.* Harare. College Press. 1985.
―――― *The Eagle and the Chickens and Other Stories.* Kenya. Tana Press. 1986.
―――― *Birds and Other Poems.* Harare. College Press. 1987.
―――― *Changes: a Love Story.* New York. The Women's Press. 1991.
―――― *An Angry Letter in January.* New York. Dangaroo Press. 1992.
―――― *The Girl Who Can and Other Stories.* London. Heinemann. African Writers Series. 1997.
―――― *Diplomatic Pounds & Other Stories.* Banbury. Ayebia Clarke Publishing. 2012.
―――― *After the Ceremonies.* Lincoln. University of Nebraska Press. 2017.
Arndt, Susan. "The Longevity of Whiteness and Ama Ata Aidoo's Our Sister Killjoy". *Essays in Honour of Ama Ata Aidoo at 70. A Reader in African Cultural Studies.* Ed. Anne V. Adams. Banbury. Ayebia Clarke Publishing Limited. 2012. pp. 110–121.
Atta, Sefi. *A Bit of Difference.* Northampton. Interlink Books. 2013.
Ayim, Nana Oforiatta. *The God Child.* London. Bloomsbury. Cassava Republic. 2019.
Conrad, Joseph. *Heart of Darkness.* Norton Critical Edition. Ed. Roger Kimbrough. 3rd. ed. New York. Norton.
Emecheta, Buchi. *In the Ditch.* London. Heineman. 1972.
―――― *Second Class Citizen.* New York. George Braziller. 1974.
Frank, Katherine. "Women Without Men: The Feminist Novel in Africa". *Women in African Literature Today.* 15. Trenton, NJ. Africa World Press. James Currey. 1987. pp. 14–34.
Gourdine, Angeletta. *The Difference Place Makes: Gender, Sexuality, and Diaspora Identity.* Columbus. The Ohio State University Press. 2002. pp. 80–102.
Gyasi, Yaa. *Homegoing.* New York. Vintage Books. 2016.
―――― *Transcendent Kingdom.* New York. Alphred A. Knopf. 2020.
Hoeller, Hildegard. "Ama Ata Aidoo's 'Heart of Darkness'". *Research in African Literatures.* Vol. 35. No. 1. 2004. pp. 130–147.
Needham, Anuradha Dingwaney. "An Interview with Ama Ata Aidoo". Massachusetts Review Vol. 36. No. 1. 1995. 123–133.
Nwanko, Chimalum. "The Feminist Impulse and Social Realism in Ama Ata Aidoo's *No Sweetness Here* and *Our Sister Killjoy*". *Nagambika. Studies of Women in African Literature.* Ed. Carol Boyce Davies and Anne Adams Graves. Trenton, NJ. Africa World Press. 1986. pp. 151–159.
Odamtten, Vincent O. *The Art of Ama Ata Aidoo. Polylectics and Reading Against Neocolonialism.* Gainsville. University Press of Florida. 1994.
Sackeyfio, Rose. "Altered Spaces: Interrogating Tradition and Modernity in Ama Ata Aidoo's Changes". *Obsidian: Literature of the African Diaspora.* Vol. 8. No. 2. 2007. pp. 73–93.

Selasi, Taiye. *Ghana Must Go*. New York. Penguin Press. 2013.
Wilentz. Gay. "The Politics of Exile: Reflections of A Black-Eyed Squint in *Our Sister Killjoy*". Emerging Perspectives *on Ama Ata Aidoo*. Ed. Ada Uzoamaka Azodo and Gay Wilentz. Trenton, NJ. Africa World Press. 1999. pp. 79–92.
Yang, Haiping. "Transnationality and Its Critique: Narrative Tropes of 'Borderland' in Our Sister Killjoy". *Emerging Perspectives on Ama Ata Aidoo*. Ed. Ada Uzoamaka Azodo and Gay Wilentz. Trenton, NJ. Africa World Press. 1999. pp. 93–124.

3 Violated bodies and displaced identities in Chika Unigwe's *on Black Sisters' Street*

Chika Unigwe's oeuvre is situated among an array of leading women writers from Nigeria in the twenty-first century. Recognized as a 'third-generation' writer, her fiction resonates with the novels of other successful contemporary authors such as Chimamanda Ngozi Adichie, Sefi Atta, NoViolet Bulawayo, Taiye Selasi, and Yaa Gyasi among others who write diaspora fiction. Unigwe's writing has won critical international acclaim; she was the winner of Africa's largest literary award, the Nigeria Prize for Literature in 2012 for *On Black Sisters' Street* (2009). This chapter engages the complexities of the international sex industry through the multi-voiced perceptions of four African women. The intersection of local and global forces creates a pattern of ruinous outcomes and, through their collective voices, they chronicle the struggle to overcome adversity, patriarchal control, and ethnic conflict.

On Black Sisters' Street is a vivid account of the ways in which the post-colonial landscape in Africa may crush women's dreams of self-fulfillment and success. Chika Unigwe has published other notable works such as *Phoenix* (2007), *Night Dancer* (2012) and *The Black Messiah* (2013), which reimagines the inner world of the historic ex-slave Olaudah Equiano. Her latest fictional work is a collection of interrelated stories, *Better Never Than Late* (2019). Unigwe has also published two early collections of poetry *Tear Drops* (1993) and *Born in Nigeria* (1995).

Much of 'third-generation' African literature by women engages diaspora themes in ways that explore women's experiences within multi-local spaces in the West. Unigwe writes from first-hand knowledge of the diaspora experiences of Nigerian migrants in Belgium, where she lived for almost two decades. Her novels *On Black Sisters' Street*, *Phoenix*, and short story collection *Better Never Than Late* are set against the Belgium landscape and offer compelling and insightful portraits of shifting identities, patriarchal structures, and racial encounters among

DOI: 10.4324/9781003219323-4

other salient themes. In a 2013 interview in Belgium with Elisabeth Bekers, Unigwe discusses her diaspora perspective abroad and notes: "Distance helps you see better" (2015: 30). *On Black Sisters' Street* presents the skillfully crafted rendering of the transnational gaze on African women's lives on the continent as well as their problematic identities in Belgium. In the novel, the author's 'gaze' encapsulates the modalities of social, economic, and political forces in the lives of African women as they emerge as transnational subjects in Europe.

An important feature of third-generation African women's writing is the exploration of new and timely themes such as sex trafficking, violence against women, war and ethnic conflict, hybridity, and mobility. The literature of contemporary women writers has reconfigured the direction of the African novel in the global age. Similar to Chika Unigwe, other contemporary female authors that examine unsavory outcomes for women battling adversity are Sefi Atta in *Swallow* (2010) and her short story "Last Trip" from her collection *News From Home* (2010). In these works, young Nigerian women make desperate choices to become drug smugglers between Nigeria and London. Akachi Adimora Ezeigbo's *Trafficked* (2008) portrays a Nigerian woman who falls prey to sex traffickers, but who eventually escapes and returns to Nigeria. Very importantly, local and global dynamics play havoc in the fertile soil of poverty, gender inequality, patriarchy, and overall economic malaise in the Nigerian environment, and women and girls are the most vulnerable in society.

On Black Sisters' Street presents the stories of four young African women, three of whom are from Nigeria and one from Sudan. Despite the diverse nature of their lives in Africa, they are linked as sex workers in Belgium as part of the dark underbelly of global mobility for African migrant women. The authentic flavor of the work represents art imitating life, because in Belgium Unigwe's research for the novel included interviews with African prostitutes in the infamous red-light district in Antwerp. The novel is a cautionary tale that portends a questionable and uncertain future for vulnerable African women enmeshed in crushing poverty, dangerous circumstances, and myriad societal constraints.

The novel unfolds the observations of the narrator in ways that foreground the spatio-temporal dimensions of Africa and Belgium, the past and the present, and the hybrid identities of the women who inhabit both worlds. The Nigerian women are Sisi, Ama, and Efe, and Alek from Sudan. Unigwe displays duality of the migrant female subject through two characters that acquire different names in Belgium. Chisom becomes Sisi while Alek becomes Joyce, as the women assume identities as prostitutes with no legal status in Belgium. The hybrid spaces of their lives elaborate the transitional elements of uprooted identities and the sadness it invokes in the women. The novel moves back and forth in time to create an elliptical narrative arc with Sisi at the center. Sadly, her life, and death convey dark undertones of the work and illustrate that migrant women's bodies are a disposable commodity in the Belgium sex industry.

The post-independence landscape of Lagos is the setting in the beginning of *On Black Sisters' Street*, along with many classic Nigerian novels in the mid twentieth century. Lagos features prominently in works among first-generation writers, as well as third-generation authors in the global age. Notable among these is Cyprian Ekwensi's *People of the City* (1954), and *Jagua Nana* (1961), as well as Achebe's *No Longer at Ease* (1960), Wole Soyinka's *The Interpreters* (1965), and *The Joys of Motherhood* (1979) by Buchi Emecheta. The Lagos novel in the twenty-first century includes Chris Abani's *Graceland* (2004), Chimamanda Ngozi Adichie's *Purple Hibiscus* (2005), and later *Americanah* (2013), along with Nnedi Okorafor's *Lagoon* (2016). Additionally, Sefi Atta's two novels, *Everything Good Will Come* (2005) and *Swallow* (2010) and her short story "Last Trip" from her collection *News from Home* (2010) are set in the Lagos metropolis. Chris Dunton notes the importance of the urban setting because "Lagos, has by the early years of the twenty-first century become established as one of the world's preeminent fictionalized cities, as with London and Paris more than a hundred years before" (2008: 3).

Nigeria became independent from Great Britain in 1962, with Lagos as the former capital of Africa's most populous nation that became the site of post-colonial exuberance and buoyant hopes for nation-building. Despite enormous wealth from oil revenues, Nigeria's development is riddled with political instability, corruption, mismanagement, and economic policies that undermine growth potential for the nation from the late twentieth century into the global age. Nevertheless, Lagos is a sprawling, dynamic metropolis, and Oniwe aptly describes the megacity as the "nerve center of all the important national activities ... as well as its representation as "a hybrid of chaos and order" (2015: 125). In many fictional works that are set in Lagos, characters experience the deleterious and corrupting influence of the city and end up with fractured lives, questionable occupations, and moral corruption.

Further, Chris Dunton succinctly identifies the potentially injurious influences of Lagos in early as well as contemporary novels by Nigerian writers:

> The documentation and exploration of severe economic and social problems remains as much a concern of the contemporary Lagos

novel as it was for Ekwensi fifty years ago. In many respects that concern has become more urgent, as the city's problems –and the ways in which these problems reflect dysfunction within the Nigerian state as a whole-have become more monstrous.

(2008: 71)

On Black Sisters' Street is not a 'Lagos novel' since much of the setting is in Belgium. Nevertheless, the city is an epicenter in the lives of the four women characters, because their journeys abroad begin in Lagos where they are recruited as sex workers. The Lagos environment is a seductive, nocuous, and magnetic entity in the way that women are drawn into a web of lies and deceit that leads to prostitution abroad. Elizabeth Olaoye (2015: 136) examines the influence of the city on the "psyche and bodies of female characters" in Sefi Atta's novels that parallel the women's vulnerability and desperation in *On Black Sisters' Street*. The fabric of the work offers carefully nuanced portraits of the challenging circumstances of each woman as well as to trace their eventual journey into sex slavery. A common denominator in the women's experiences is meeting Dele, the pimp who trafficks them to Europe.

Sackeyfio notes that:

> *On Black Sisters' Street* goes beyond descriptions of the unwholesome nature of the sex trade to also reveal how patriarchal structures, poverty and desperation lead to unwise choices among the restricted opportunities for women to survive by legitimate means. The four women characters arrive in Belgium around the same time and gradually draw closer as they cope with their circumstances. They end up telling their stories as a cathartic experience of sisterhood. The centrality of the female narrative voice evokes the reader's insight into the inner world of the women's subjectivity. In this way, the women are humanized figures that are treated with compassion.
>
> (2014: 202)

Unigwe has crafted a finely sketched portrait of Sisi as a university graduate in Lagos. Her name is Chisom and she dreamed of leaving Lagos because "This place has no future ... She tried not to breathe too deeply because doing so would be inhaling the stench of mildewed dreams" (2009: 18). Of all the women characters she is the only one who is educated and her family has invested all their hopes in her for a bright future. Her father instills the mantra: "The only way to a better life is education. *Awukwo*. Face your books and the sky will be your limit" (18).

> She studied hard at school, mindful of her father's hopes for her: a good job once she graduated from the University of Lagos. She had envisaged her four years of studying Finance and Business Administration culminating, quite logically, in a job with a bank, one of those new banks dotting Lagos like a colony of palm trees.
>
> (2009: 20)

Sadly, Sisi never gets a job and the mounting frustration is crippling her so that sometimes she imagined that her "resume's were being swallowed up by the many potholes on Lagos roads" (22). These unfortunate events represent contemporary challenges that plague untold numbers of university graduates in Nigeria and other developing nations and gender inequality exacerbates the problem for women.

The author's realism dramatizes a continuing trend of massive unemployment among Nigeria's teeming youth and the attendant suffering that ensues. Olukayode documents the alarming rate of unemployment in Nigeria at nearly 60% of the labor pool in the nation (2017: 63). Newly qualified graduates are disproportionately represented among the unemployed and "the deleterious effects on the nation's economy and affected individuals are highly unquantifiable" (64).

Unemployment continues for years as Sisi's hopes of success fade, made worse by the knowledge that some of her peers who are less qualified were employed through 'connections'. The corrupting influences of the Lagos environment take form when Sisi encounters Dele, a shrewd figure who recruits unsuspecting women into the trade. When considering his offer to help her leave Nigeria, Sisi thinks: "once she hit it big, she would reincarnate again as Chisom. She would set up a business or two. She could go into the business of importing second-hand luxury cars into Nigeria" (2009: 45). For desperate women, big dreams may lead to poor outcomes and Rasheed Olaniyi aptly notes women's vulnerability to traffickers:

> The lack of economic opportunities and the eagerness for a better life abroad has made many women and girls vulnerable to entrapment by traffickers. Traffickers entice victims to migrate voluntarily (legally) with false promises of lucrative jobs in foreign countries, as models, dancers, nannies, domestic workers and nurses ... the brokers and employers in these operations often have ties with powerful organized crime syndicates.
>
> (2003: 48)

Violated bodies and displaced identities 45

Sisi ends up in Antwerp, where her passport is taken as a routine initiation into undocumented status in Belgium because "Handing over her passport would be tantamount to putting her life into someone's else's hands ..." (2009: 119). She rationalizes that she will definitely make it in Belgium because "Lagos is a city of death and she was escaping it" (98).

Another young inhabitant of Lagos is 16-year-old Efe, whose naiveté, materialism, and poverty make her easy prey for sexual predators. After her mother dies, she is responsible for her siblings. She becomes involved with a wealthy man old enough to be her father. In exchange for sexual favors, he showers her with money, clothes, and gifts and she reflects: "Now she had Titus who was willing and able to buy her whatever she wanted" (2009: 51). Unfortunately, she gets pregnant and, following the birth of her child, she appears at his home, only to be insulted and shunned by his wife. With no support from her child's father, her only source of income is working as a cleaning woman. At her lowest point, she is working two jobs and, through an advertisement, she ends up cleaning offices for Dele. In her desperation, she hopes for a better life for herself and her child.

Like Sisi, Dele recruits Efe to travel to Europe and, naively, "she agreed to his terms before she asked what she was expected to do abroad" (2009: 82). Dele tells her that a woman can earn easy money in Belgium:

> Efe had dreamed up the riches she would amass and had calculated that she would be able to afford a Mercedes by the time she had spent a year working. And as for liking black women, Dele had told her they were in great demand by white men, tired of their women and wanting a bit of color and spice.
>
> (84).

Similar, to Sisi and Efe, Ama's early experiences in Lagos foreshadow the dark period when she is trafficked to Belgium. As a child, she endures trauma when, at age eight, she is raped by her stepfather, Brother Cyril. She is haunted for years by the continued abuse and when she finally tells her mother, her mother does not believe her and she is abruptly sent to Lagos to live with her Aunt Eko. She works in her aunt's restaurant where she meets Dele who is a customer.

Like Sisie and Efe, she is recruited to work in Europe and dreams of a better future in Belgium:

> Her thoughts already on a new life far from here, earning her own money so that she could build her business empire ... it was this

dream that spurred her on in Antwerp; the men she slept with were, like Dele just tools she needed to achieve her dream.

(2009: 169)

Unlike the other women, she is intimate with Dele in Lagos and rationalizes that selling her body in Belgium, as opposed to Lagos, would confer anonymity. While in Antwerp, the disquieting memories of her life in Nigeria are overshadowed by her transnational identity as a sex worker as her emotions harden her over time.

Alek's story expands the local dimensions of the novel beyond the pernicious environment of Lagos to include the conflict zone of Sudan. Unigwe presents Alek's horrific experience through recollection of sexual violence in her homeland and subsequent displacement across national borders in Africa and eventually Belgium. The author dramatizes the vulnerability of women to sexual violence during one of Africa's most devastating ethnic conflicts in the twenty-first century. Throughout history, women have all too often become victims and easy prey during armed conflict and their bodies used as weapons of war and the target of ethnic cleansing or outright genocide.

Moreover, "Rape, enslaved prostitution, and other sexual violence against women have been part of war for all of recorded history – across *all* cultures, and in all kinds of wars, be they religious, colonizing, or revolutionary" (Farr 2005: 165).

The war in western Sudan displaced hundreds of thousands of people, causing massive movement to refugee camps, neighboring countries, and abroad. The Darfur crisis embodied ethnic targeting of non-Arab communities engulfed in sexual violence by the Arab Janjaweed militia and the Sudanese military forces.

Unigwe's realism conveys Alek's story against the dangerous conditions of the conflict. Alek is only 15 and her family is preparing to leave their home for a refugee camp near Khartoum, and perhaps eventually migrate to the UK. Events around them had taken an alarming and threatening turn as people were disappearing amidst rumors of approaching militia forces. The unthinkable happens when the Janjaweed soldiers burst into their home and kill her parents while Alek is hiding in the cupboard. The terror is unbearable and in a moment of anger Alek bursts out of hiding to avenge her parents.

She looks at the men and thinks, "All I wanted was to be able to attack these men who had just blown my life away, as if it were a handful of dust" (2009: 190).

She is gang raped by the soldiers and referred to as an African slave. The ethnic dimensions of such assaults are confirmed in a 2008 study of the conflict titled "Racial Targeting of Sexual Violence in Darfur" by Hagan et al. who confirm:

> Combined attacks by Sudanese government forces and Janjaweed militia forces led to racial epithets being used more often during sexual victimization in Darfur. Our results suggest that the Sudanese government is participating in the use of sexual assault as a racially targeted weapon against ethnically African civilians.
>
> (19)

The physical and emotional trauma Alek experiences illustrate not only women's vulnerability in war and conflict but the potential for a downward spiral into other forms of sexual exploitation and unfavorable outcomes later in life. Disoriented and dazed, Alek ends up in a refugee camp where she hears stories worse than her own. Miserable and alienated in the refugee camp, she eventually meets Polycarp, a Nigerian soldier with the African Union Peacekeeping force. They fall in love and she accompanies him to Nigeria. Alek expects to eventually marry Polycarp but, after they had lived together for over a year, his Igbo mother visits and rudely rejects her because she is not Nigerian.

To end the relationship, Polycarp colludes with Dele to send her to Belgium as a 'nanny'. This turn of events begins Alex's descent into a bonded sex worker, a new identity, and years of exploitation. The two men essentially decide her fate as she is given a new name: "Joyce. Yes. Joyce. Dat one sound like name wey dey always jolly. Joooooyyce!" (2009: 230). Unknown to Alek, the name-change ushers her objectification and market value of her sexuality, over which she no longer has control. During the making of the arrangements, Dele and Polycarp are laughing uncontrollably while Alek is seething on the inside. Although angry, this event evokes remembrance of the night she is assaulted in Sudan: "The soldiers that raped her that night in Daru had taken her strength, and Polycarp's betrayal had left her unwilling to seek it back" (231). Her new identity is sealed by Dele and, on the journey to Belgium, she recollects that "The flight was long. And Dark. And Lonely. Alek felt like cargo with a tag: Destination Unknown. For what did she know about where she was going?" (233). After meeting Madam in Antwerp, Alek is given two days before she starts working. She promises herself that she will never depend on anyone else for her happiness.

The novel ends tragically with the death of Sisi at the hands of Segun, who represents the underworld of the Belgium mafia. She had fallen in love with one of her customers and made plans to escape and marry him. Upon news of her death the women come together to mourn, reflect on their lives, and to share their experiences. The intertwined stories of Sisi, Ama, Efe, and Joyce, first in Lagos and later as sex workers in Belgium, form a tapestry of local and global sex trafficking of African women as a mirror of exploitation and gender inequality. Chielozona Eze affirms that

> They are lured to Europe not only by the promises of the continent that colonized theirs, but more especially because of the political, social and economic dysfunction that have brought different forms of tragedy to their homelands: war, rape, poverty and political corruption.
>
> (2014: 90)

The novel skillfully illustrates the ways in which patriarchal structures in Africa entraps the women in a web of exploitation, violence, objectification, and commodification. With Dele at the center, other male characters who prey on the women are Brother Cyril, Titus, Polycarp, Sudanese soldiers and, later, Segun in Belgium.

Through Dele, each of the women is ensnared by comments such as those told to Sisi in pidgin English: "Na when you get there, begin work, you go begin dey pay. Instalmental payment we dey call am! Mont' by mont'you go dey pay me" (2009: 35). He objectifies her by describing her body: "see your backside, *kai*! As for those melons wey you carry for chest, *omo,* how you no go fin'work?" (43). Likewise, when Efe is approached by Dele and asks about the kind of work she will do in Belgium, she is told 'sales' as he looks at her body. Further, Olaniyi notes that *On Black Sisters' Street* evokes the trans-Atlantic slave trade that lasted over 300 years, and calls this form of modern-day trafficking, "Slaves of the new millennium" (2003: 49). Sexual objectification represents the male 'gaze' that dehumanizes women, who are reduced to marketable subjects, reminiscent of slave auctions where captives were examined and assessed for their perceived market value as human cargo. As in chattel slavery, men are the owners of women's bodies as personal property in the global arena. Olaniyi elaborates the power of males to control women's sexuality as part of the web of societal factors that codify women's subordinate status and vulnerability to trafficking:

> Unequal gender relations and patriarchal values underlie women trafficking. I argue that trafficking in women is another manifestation of patriarchal and familial control over female labor and sexuality. Under globalization patriarchy has crossed the frontiers of public space into the international arena. Women

are experiencing heightened levels of exploitation, insecurity, vulnerability, poverty and illiteracy. Globalization as pauperized women by its expansion of the sex industry, keeping them in perpetual slavery and penury.

(46)

After the women arrive in Belgium they are handed over to a 'madam', who ironically is educated. As part of the international crime syndicate Madam is no less cruel than Dele and quickly assumes total control over the newly arrived women. She commands Sisi and each of the women to "hand over your passport. From now until your debt is paid I am in charge of it" (2009: 119). These developments highlight the insidious nature of these conditions as a form of modern-day slavery. Ejalu examines the strategies of bonded sex labor and states that:

> Upon arriving in the destination country, traffickers typically confiscate their victims' documents and force their victims to remain in servitude until their contract- which can be tens of thousands of dollars-is paid off. During such servitude, victims often incur more debt because traffickers will frequently charge them for necessary expenses like food, rent, and visits to the doctor. Thus begins an endless cycle of debt and bondage.

(2006: 168)

Furthermore, Olaniyi posits that "the trafficking of Nigerian women into slavery and debt bondage in the global sex industry occurs within the larger global context of economic and social trends" (2003: 46). When Sisi returns from a failed attempt to gain asylum at immigration headquarters, Madam reminds her sharply: "you're a persona non grata in this country. You do not exist. Not here" (2003: 182). These comments cement her status as a trafficked woman who must pay off her debt. Madam tells her:

> Now, until you have paid up every single kobo ... every single cent of what you owe us, you will not have your passport back. Every month we expect five hundred euros from you ... Every month you go to the Western Union and transfer the money to Dele. Any month you do not pay up ... She let the threat hang, unspoken.

(2009: 183)

One can only imagine the accumulated wealth of individuals like Dele who function within complex and far-reaching international crime networks. Sisi, Ama, Joyce, and Efe describe Dele's wealth and, because of Nigeria's devalued currency, his profits are multiplied significantly in Lagos. Although women like Madam will profit from sex labor as well, the industry is a male-dominated sphere; hence patriarchal hierarchies and domains of power prevail and constitute a formidable international system of market-driven forces.

In sum, the women in Chika Unigwe's *On Black Sisters' Street* speak with one voice to narrate their pain, dehumanization, and tragedy. The social, economic, and political failures of the post-colonial state wreak havoc in the lives of women and forecast bleak futures for legitimate means of survival. In Nigeria, and across the African continent, neoliberal policies of the late twentieth century resulted in uneven development and severe economic hardship for the masses, and precipitated a downward spiral into economic malaise, leaving women in the margins of the labor pool. Nigerian women's marginalized status and subordination through sociocultural norms were exacerbated through the dramatic decline of employment opportunities in society. Moreover, the setting of the novel crosses borders to Sudan to examine ethnic conflict as a cause of displacement and ultimately trafficking to Europe among women.

Trapped in desperate circumstances, the lure of migration abroad illustrates the dynamics of the economic divide between the global north and African nations.

The novel brings to life the complexities of the international sex industry drawn from fictional accounts of African sex workers in Antwerp as transnational subjects. The experiences the women endure represent both local and global dimensions of women's oppression that juxtapose the Atlantic slave trade and modern-day slavery. Through the female characters, women's lives in Africa represent a conflation of challenging circumstances that predispose their unwise choices.

Ironically, the woman who loses her life in Belgium is educated and her story illustrates the convergence of political corruption, failed economic policies, and familial conventions to cloud her future. Although the women's backgrounds are diverse, marginality, poverty and patriarchal norms are connecting threads of their involvement in the sex industry. Patriarchy is an overarching force in the lives of African women in the novel and, even when there is no outright violence against a female, male authority in society may exact compliance, silence, and obedience from women.

On Black Sisters' Street vividly conveys the unwholesome and potentially injurious landscape of Lagos for Nigerian women. Limited opportunities for economic stability reduce women to potential victims in the shadowy environment of corruption among unsavory characters in Lagos to heighten local dimensions of the work. Unigwe's portrayal of Lagos expresses similar features with those of many Nigerian novelists in the past, as well as in contemporary works. Patriarchal networks emerge in the global arena to exert control of women's labor and sexuality. *On Black Sisters' Street* is a caveat in the global age of mobility and mass displacement. Unigwe has given voice to the untold stories of women's lives in the shadowy underworld of sex trafficking between Nigeria and Belgium. Given the dearth of literary texts and research on sex trafficking from Africa relative to other populations in the world, *On Black Sisters' Street* is an insightful and invaluable representation of commodification of black women's bodies in the global sex industry.

Works cited

Abani, Chris. *Graceland*. New York. Picador. 2004.
Achebe, Chinua. *No Longer at Ease*. London. Heineman. 1960.
Adichie, Chimamanda Ngozi. *Purple Hibiscus*. Lagos. Farafina. 2004.
―――― *Americanah*. Toronto. Alfred A. Knopf. 2013.
Atta, Sefi. *Everything Good Will Come*. Northampton. Interlink Books. 2005.
―――― *News from Home*. Northampton, Interlink Books, 2010.
―――― *Swallow*. Northampton. Interlink Books. 2010.
Bekers, Elisabeth. "Writing Africa in Belgium, Europe: A Conversation with Chika Unigwe". *Research in African Literatures*. Vol. 46. No. 4. 2015. pp. 26–34.
Dunton, Chris. "Entropy and Energy: Lagos as city of Words". *Research in African Literatures*. Vol. 39. No. 2. 2008. pp. 68–78.
Ejalu, William A.E. "From Home to Hell". *Trafficking and the Global Sex Industry*. Ed. Karen Beeks and Delila Amir. Lanham, MD. Lexington Books. 2006.
Ekwensi, Cyprian. *Jagua Nana*. London. Heinemann. 1961.
―――― *People of the City*. London. Heinemann. 1963.
―――― *News from Home*. Northampton. Interlink Books. 2010.
Emecheta, Buchi. *The Joys of Motherhood*. London. Allison and Busby. 1979.
Eze, Chielozona. "Feminism with a Big 'F': Ethics and the Rebirth of African Feminism in Chika Unigwe's On Black Sisters' Street". *Research in African Literatures*. Vol. 45. No. 4. 2014. pp. 89–103.
Ezeigbo, Akachi Adimora, *Trafficked*. Lagos. Lantern Books. 2008.
Farr, Kathryn. *Sex Trafficking: The Global Market in Women and Children*. New York. Worth Publishers. 2005.
Habila, Helon. *Waiting for an Angel*. London. Penguin. 2004.
Hagan, John et al. "Racial Targeting of Sexual Violence in Darfur". *American Journal of Public Health*. Vol. 99. No. 1386_2392. doi.org/10.2105/AJPH.2008. 141119.
Okorafor, Nnedi. *Lagoon*. New York. Saga Press. 2016.

Olaniyi, Rasheed. "No Way Out: The Trafficking of Women in Nigeria." *Agenda*. Vol. 55. 2003. pp. 101–116.

Olaoye, Elizabeth. "The Influence of Lagos on Women in Sefi Atta's Novels". *Writing Contemporary Nigeria. How Sefi Atta Illuminates African Culture and Tradition.* Ed. Walter P. Collins, III. Amherst, MA. Cambria. 2015. pp. 135–153.

Olukayode, Longe. "Graduate Unemployment in Nigeria: Causes, Consequences and Remedial Approaches". *American Journal of Contemporary Research*. Vol. 7. No. 4. 2017. pp. 63–73.

Oniwe, Bernard. "Images and Voices of Lagos in Sefi Atta's Lagos Novels". *Writing Contemporary Nigeria. How Sefi Atta Illuminates African Culture and Tradition.* Ed. Walter P. Collins, III. Amherst, MA. Cambria. 2015. pp. 121–133.

Sackeyfio, Rose. "Black Women's Bodies in a Global Economy: Sex, Lies and Slavery" *At The CrossRoads: Readings of the Postcolonial and the Global in African Literature and Visual Art*. Ed. Ghirmai Negash, Andrea Frohne and Samuel Zadi. Trenton, NJ. Africa World Press. 2014. pp. 199–210.

Soyinka, Wole. *The Interpreters.* London. Heinemann. 1965.

Unigwe, Chika. *Tear Drops.* Enugu. Richardson Publishers. 1993.

——— *Born in Nigeria.* Enugu. Onyx Publishers. 1995.

——— *Phoenix.* Lagos. Farafina Trust. 2007.

——— *On Black Sisters' Street.* London. Jonathan Cape. 2009.

——— *Night Dancer.* London. Jonathan Cape. 2012.

——— *Black Messiah.* Dutch Translation. *De Zwarte Messias.* Trans. Hans van Riemsdijit. Antwerp. De Bezige. 2013.

——— *Better Never Than Late.* Abuja. Cassava Republic. 2019.

4 Negotiating identity and Pan-African aesthetics in *Americanah* by Chimamanda Ngozi Adichie

Chimamanda Ngozi Adichie is Africa's brightest new star in the literary world, and her fiction has won critical acclaim, establishing her as Africa's most celebrated contemporary writer. In recent years, Adichie's creative artistry has offered critical insight into twenty-first century landscapes of African identity within transnational spaces in the global age. This chapter examines Adichie's explorations of race, identity, and Pan-Africanism through a gendered lens in *Americanah* (2013). Her novel addresses racialized identities within a Pan-African framework of diaspora sojurn in the West. Adichie's novel will be examined through an African-centered framework of literary Pan-Africanism, conceptualized by African American scholar, Christel N. Temple in 2004.

Adichie's life mirrors *Americanah*'s protagonist because she migrated from Nigeria at age 19 to pursue education in America. Through a meteoric rise to celebrity, she has emerged as a leading figure and spokesperson among third-generation African writers. Her education began with a scholarship to study communications at Drexel University and she continued at Eastern Connecticut University where she completed a BA in 2001. At Johns Hopkins Adichie earned a Master's Degree in Creative Writing.

Adichie's rise to fame began with her first novel *Purple Hibiscus* (2004), which became an award-winning bestseller, followed by her epic narrative of the Nigeria–Biafra War in *Half of a Yellow Sun* (2006). In 2009 she published a collection of short stories, *The Thing Around Your Neck* and her latest novel, *Americanah* (2013), explores the dynamics of race, hybridity, and transnationalism in the lives of Nigerian immigrants in the USA and the UK. Adichie's writing interrogates and (re)imagines the new as well as old perceptions of African encounters with the West.

As an influential figure in the literary world, Adichie's ideas on women's and gender identities and experiences have sparked controversy and debate. She articulates contemporary perceptions of gender

DOI: 10.4324/9781003219323-5

dynamics in two collections of essays: *We Should All Be Feminists* (2015) and *Dear Ijeawelwe* or: *A Feminist Manifesto in Fifteen Suggestions* (2017). The National Academy of Arts and Letters bestowed recognition on Adichie as Foreign Honorary Member (2017) for her distinguished contributions to literature. Noted as a remarkable new talent from Nigeria, she has joined the constellation of world-renowned literary icons. On the cover of *Half of a Yellow Sun* (2007), the late Chinua Achebe praised Adichie's work: "We do not usually associate wisdom with beginners, but here is a new writer endowed with the gift of ancient storytellers ... Adichie came almost fully made." Achebe's tribute to Adichie's talent symbolizes her importance as a writer whose influence spans the boundaries of the Igbo nation, Nigeria, Africa, and the literary world.

Adichie is the winner of numerous prestigious and distinguished awards for her writing, such as the O. Henry Prize (2003), the Commonwealth Writer's Prize (2005), and the Orange Prize in 2007. Adichie received the MacArthur Genius Fellowship (2008) for *Purple Hibiscus* and she won the Hurston/Wright Legacy award (2004) for best debut work, and the National Book Critics Circle in 2013, for *Americanah*. In 2010 she was listed among the *New Yorker*'s "20 Under 40" and is noted among the "100 Most Influential Africans for 2013".

Adichie's novel *Americanah* and short stories from her collection, *The Thing Around Your Neck* examine the complexities of African diaspora subjectivity for immigrants who traverse geographical, linguistic, and ethnic boundaries. Her literature is part of a burgeoning corpus of African diaspora fiction that foreground hybridity as a salient theme within the works of African writers educated and based in the West.

Her writing is also an enormous contribution to post-colonial writing, world literature, and women's writing in ways that shape the development of African literature in the global age. As a voice for third-generation African writers, Adichie's perspectives on a broad range of themes such as identity, transnationalism, culture, gender, and literature augments discourse about Africa and the African diaspora in the twenty-first century. Adichie is listed among a new crop of African writers whose literary corpus is concerned with nomadism, exile, displacement, and deracination (Adesani and Dunton 2005: 16).

Americanah may be conceptualized as a treatise on race and, to begin, Adichie conveys her displeasure and rejection of being labeled *black* in America. In an insightful interview called: "Learning To Be Black in The US", originally broadcast on NPR in 2013, she recalls that growing up in Nigeria, she was never identified by the color of her skin and she states candidly:

I think that one is not burdened by America's terrible racial history, and I think when people say to me, "You're different. You're not angry", in some ways it also feels that I'm being made complicit for something that I don't want to be complicit in. Because in some ways they're saying, "You're one of the good ones." And I think to say that is to somehow ignore the reality of American history. And they'll tell me some story of some African-American woman they knew who just wasn't like me. Which I find quite absurd.

(NPR 2013: 4)

These ideas, spoken very passionately, strike at the heart of the complexity of racial discourse in the diaspora among African and African diaspora communities whose experiences are not shared, but are rather shaped by contradistinctive historical, cultural, and geographical contexts. The absence of historical context, either by African immigrants, Caucasians, or diaspora people themselves, illustrates the great chasm among communities of color caused by ignorance, bias, and historical amnesia. Adichie admits her ignorance before migrating to America and in another interview called "Race doesn't occur to me" with Aaron Bady, she describes how she 'learned' to be black in America. She recalls that even though she had not been in the country long, she already knew that to be 'black' was not a good thing in America, and she did not want to be 'black' (Boston Review 2014: 7.)

She generalizes these sentiments to other black immigrants from Africa and the Caribbean. Further, Adichie shares that "it took about a year of reading, learning, watching, for me to really come around and realize that there's a context-you know, I read American history and I'm just amazed at how recent some of the things that happened were" (Boston Review 2014: 7). Within a dialogic framework, these issues have yet to be aired and discussed systematically and collectively to facilitate truth, healing, and reconciliation that will forge productive relationships among Africans and African diaspora people. Adichie, in refusing complicity in racially divisive postures, acknowledges the reality of *blackness* when in the USA and explores her ideas in her novel *Americanah*. Adichie's positionality with regard to racial identity in America is instructive in ways that resonate fundamental 'truths' about history, stereotypes, ignorance, and divisiveness in the black world.

In crafting her runaway bestseller *Americanah*, published in 2013, Adichie's literary imagination illustrates the author's use of her creative artistry to (re)frame and to reposition the discourse of race and identity in America through the lens of gender. Through multiple diaspora settings, a broad range of characters represent the complexities of immigrant experiences of fragmented identity and debilitating experiences in the struggle to survive. *Americanah* succeeds on various levels, first as a panoramic love story that spans Nigeria, America and the UK. Secondly, the portrayal of African immigrant experiences creates a skillfully woven tapestry of cultural hybridity, alienation, and otherness within transnational spaces of the West. The Nigerian characters navigate the discomfort of racialized identities against the backdrop of poverty, depression, and challenges to their dignity and humanity. Finally, *Americanah* effectively captures the intersection of race, class, and gender through the narrative voice of Ifemelu, who awakens to sexuality and to her vulnerability as a female struggling to survive in a hostile environment.

The title, *Americanah,* is a Nigerian colloquial expression that denotes a person who has gone to America and returned with American affectations, mannerisms, and pretense of newly acquired sophistication. The experiences of Ifemelu, the female protagonist, share similarities to Adichie's life when she came to America to pursue her education. Ifemelu's journey into the realities of Western life is a coming-of-age chronicle of the search for 'self' amidst paradoxical experiences of otherness and marginality. The novel is a vivid rendering of the ways in which African immigrants are forced to negotiate the politics of race and identity as they encounter America's obsession with *blackness* as the legacy of slavery and distorted perceptions of 'racial others'. American constructions of race are a major theme in the work, and the interrogation of the dichotomy between Africans and African Americans unfold the Pan-African elements of the author's worldview.

Adichie explores diverse observations about race in America through Ifemelu's blog, which is very successful. With reference to the blog, Miriam Pahl notes: "The blog Adichie creates for Ifemelu inside the novel exhibits a strong political commitment. It negotiates the hierarchization of cultures and criticizes white-centeredness of the US environment depicted in the novel, and chronicles everyday incidents of racism (2016: 77–78). Adichie describes her motivation to include the blogging element in her novel: "I wanted this novel to also be social commentary, but I wanted to say it in ways that are different from what one is supposed to say in literary fiction" (quoted in Adichie and Rifbjerg. The blog is called "Raceteenth or Various Observations About American Blacks (Those Formerly Known as Negroes) by a Non-American Black". Sackeyfio observes that:

> One of the most provocative postings is called 'To My Fellow Non-American Blacks: In America, You Are Black Baby'. The

articulation of this dilemma experienced by immigrants is one of the novels most compelling messages. By giving voice to these perceptions, Adichie addresses the *elephant in the room* that compounds the novel's realism. The racialized environment of America and other western nations imposes *blackness* as an all-consuming identity without recognition of ethnicity or difference.

(2013: 15)

Ifemelu addresses her fellow African immigrants in the blog:

> Dear Non-American Black, when you make the choice to come to America, you become black. Stop arguing. Stop saying I'm Jamaican or I'm Ghanaian. America doesn't care. So what if you weren't 'black' in your country? You're in America now. We all have our initiation into the society of former Negroes.
>
> (2013: 222)

The inclusion of the word "we" suggests solidarity, not only among immigrant communities but affiliation with the *old* African diaspora as well. These ideas represent shared history as a basic underpinning of Pan-Africanism. All populations of black people have experienced forms of oppression and exploitation by Europeans through slavery, colonization, imperialism, religion, environmental exploitation, and, in the twenty-first century, globalization. Although these sentiments do not translate to political solidarity within a larger framework, it indicates commonality based on race within a mutually hostile environment. Whether or not African immigrants chafe against being identified as black, the reality of their perceived *blackness* by the majority race is inescapable and certainly shapes their experiences in the West. Thus, Adichie's Pan-Africanist stance is clear in her recognition of historical contexts and the attendant realities of racism. The ideas expressed in the blog reflect her attempt to understand racial dynamics in America as a basis for future interaction between African Americans and African immigrants. These perceptions are supported by Adichie's year-long research on American history and her expressions of admiration for the resilience of African Americans throughout centuries of oppression. Cheryl Sterling summarizes these realities by reminding us that:

> Fanon famously states, "wherever the Negro goes, the Negro remains a Negro" and, at least in the U.S. the police affirm this truism. I cannot help but speculate that if Amadou Diallo when hailed with 41 bullets and Ousmane Zongo in his storage locker,

had shouted: "I'm not Black", would it have changed any aspect of their deaths? One can shoot in the air or at many different parts of the body to stop an individual, but when all of the shots directed at the Black body are meant to kill then the naming of the reality of racism and interpretation of racialized subjectivity has to come together, and Pan-Africanist discourse does this.

(2015: 128)

Regardless of ethnic diversity and historical specificity throughout the black world, the acknowledgement of racialized identities is a precondition for meaningful dialog and mutual understanding between the old and new diaspora communities.

In looking closely at expressions of Pan-Africanism in *Americanah*, Christel N. Temple's publication, *Literary Pan-Africanism: History, Contexts, and Criticism* (2004) is an appropriate analytical model. The work is a significant contribution to literary studies and the conceptual framework explicates and extends the fundamental tenets of Pan-Africanism to the analysis of literary texts by African writers. The premise of the book expands the epistemological underpinnings of a body of literature that, like all constructions of literary theory, is one of many operable ways to approach a text.

The use of Pan-Africanism as an analytical framework is African-centered, at the same time that it remains cognizant of diverse historical experiences and the complexities of theorizations of black/African unity in the global age of transformation and flux and shifting identities. Nyamnjoh and Shoro pose the question of what it means to write in a Pan-African manner and they acknowledge that there is no simple answer. Literary Pan-Africanism attempts to identify the "extent to which African writers have embraced and promoted Pan-Africanism, and examines how open and inclusive they have been in this regard" (2011: 3). Christel N. Temple has developed a conceptual structure that outlines seven major criteria that constitute an African-centered paradigm of Pan-African literary criticism:

> The text seeks to generate relationships, historical understandings, and future interaction between Africans and the descendants of the Africans dispersed through the European enslavement; (b) The writer introduces mutual understanding and nurtures the relationship between Africans and African Americans; (c) The philosophy and ideals of the narrative parallel tenets of contemporary and/ or traditional Pan-African ideology; (d) Texts of this category utilize similar terminology expressive of a return, that consistently

demonstrates the usage of the prefix *re*. (e)The African American characters are generally non-stereotyped depictions; (f) the author's social, cultural, political and/or ideological deliberateness is pan-African, Afrocentric, and/or African centered; and finally, (g) The author usually has spent time among African American communities in the United States.

(2004: 4)

The following discussion explores the ways in which characters and salient themes, as expressed in *Americanah*, successfully project Adichie's engagement with race and identity within the tenets of literary Pan-Africanism.

Americanah unfolds Ifemelu's coming of age to the social construction of 'race' in the USA in ways that fulfills the tenets of Pan-Africanism. The sense of unity with other black people appears early in the novel, when Ifemelu is getting her hair braided in a salon peopled by women from Mali and Senegal, and where she is made to feel welcome as a fellow West African. Also, Ifemelu experiences strong affinity with her aunt's neighbor who is from Grenada and recalls how she and Jane "laughed when they discovered how similar their childhoods in Grenada and Nigeria had been, with Enid Blyton books, and Anglophile teachers" (2013: 112). One of the most vivid illustrations of Pan-African solidarity occurs when Ifemelu is in college and meets a group of African students. The students are from Nigeria, Uganda, Kenya, Ghana, South Africa, Tanzania, Zimbabwe, the Democratic Republic of Congo, and Guinea. In a conversation, a student from Kenya tells her: "African American is what we call our brothers and sisters whose ancestors were slaves" (141). She is advised to:

> Try and make friends with our African-American brothers and sisters in a spirit of true pan-Africanism. But make sure you remain friends with fellow Africans, as this will help you keep your perspective. Always attend African Students Association meetings, but if you must, you can also try the Black Student Union.
>
> (141)

Ifemelu learns that African Americans come to the meetings of the African students and, although some of them romanticize Africa, she is told that others might connect with her. Adichie's insights are realistic and vivid and display openness to a range of possibilities across the boundaries of historical circumstance and discontinuity in the black world. These examples capture Pan-Africanisms' requisite to regenerate and nurture relationships among Africans and African Americans irrespective of their spatio-temporal environment.

Moreover, non-stereotypical portraiture of an African American male appears in *Americanah*. Blaine is a professor at Princeton, and a skillfully etched character, with whom Ifemelu has a three-year relationship. Their relationship is stable, positive, and nurturing. Ifemelu's decision to return to Nigeria signals the end of their relationship and, consistent with Pan-African principles, the idea of 'return' to Africa brings Ifemelu's journey full circle. The decision to return to Nigeria positions Africa at the center, a clear negation of Afropolitanism's claim that an immigrant feels at 'home' in many places. An important parallel in the novel is that Obinze, Ifemelu's childhood sweetheart, has also returned home to Nigeria, albeit through deportation, and he becomes very successful.

Chimamanda Ngozi Adiche has articulated a clear stance on Pan-Africanism through numerous interviews and online postings. Additionally, in her fictional works, she presents thematic exploration of racial dynamics in America and relationships between African and African Diaspora characters that reflect Pan-African expressions. In a number of interviews, she expresses her outspoken allegiance to ideas of racial solidarity. For example, when asked by Trevor Noah whether her novel, *Americanah* is a Pan-Africanist book, she states the following:

> I think of myself politically as Pan-African ... And for me, that means I care about what's happening in Kenya, I care about the people in Bahia, Brazil, I care about Afro-Columbia, because there's a familiarity there to something I feel connected to.

She notes that: "for the diaspora as a whole, our common identity isn't based solely on our skin color" (Adichie 2005). These ideas represent Adichie's acknowledgement of solidarity with African descended peoples, regardless of the multi-local spaces, and historical and cultural specificities of the worldwide African diaspora. In a 2018 interview with Hope Reese, called "I Became Black", Adichie identifies with African Americans:

> Looking back, especially my first year in U.S., my insistence on being Nigerian, or even African, was, in many ways, my way of avoiding blackness. It's also my acknowledgement of American racism, which is to say that if blackness were benign, I would not have been running away from it.
>
> (JSTOR Daily 2018)

She narrates that after reading American history, "it made me start claiming this blackness. I went full circle and started identifying as Black".

These declarations are laudable, considering the dichotomy and pervasive tensions between Africans born on the continent and those born in the diaspora as part of the legacy of the Atlantic slave trade. Her sentiments speak to the core of historical and cultural linkages between Africa and her diaspora when she cites historical 'truth': "African American history didn't start on a slave ship, it started in Africa ... I believe there are cultural traditions that have been passed down, and diluted, but it's still there" (Adichie 2005). In stating the obvious, Adichie underscores what many people, on both sides of the Atlantic, treat with ambivalence, ignorance, and sometimes outright denial. The discourse that focuses the impact of enslavement, racial oppression, historical amnesia, and disconnection to Africa encapsulates the trauma from which both Africa and her diaspora has yet to heal. The historical dimensions of the ambiguous and frequently difficult relationship between Africa and her diaspora is a sensitive one that remains unresolved in the global age of transformation, shifting identities, and redefinition of what is means to be African.

Adichie has also expressed admiration for the resilience of African Americans, a viewpoint that is, again, unusual in the midst of critique and 'single-stories' about African Americans, especially evident in ideas related to achievement and upward mobility in America, perceived as the land of opportunity. Further, Adichie combines outspoken feminist energies and Pan-African flavor when she states: "I feel an odd pride when an Igbo, or an African American or a Nigerian does well" (Adichie Interview1). In this instance, gender solidarity with African and African diaspora women projects her consciousness of racial identity and the intersectionality of historical origins across ethnic, geographical and linguistic boundaries. The statement also foregrounds the complexities of race, class, and gender that shapes the lives of African and African diaspora women who share a background of oppression in the past as well as the present. Black women, as part of an under-represented group, prefigure what Adichie calls a sense of "we-ness" as the source of her "odd pride".

If we accept the premise of Pan-Africanism, defined by Wachira Kigotho (2016) as "the ideology that embraces the holistic historical, political, cultural, spiritual, artistic, scientific and other philosophical legacies of Africans from past times to the present", Adichie's creative artistry vividly illustrates her positive engagement with race and identity within a Pan-African framework. Further, Adichie states that

Pan-Africanism is an outlook that she came to appreciate as a result of her time abroad. She describes Nairobi as a "much calmer Lagos", and she views Jamaican culture as similar to that of (presumably coastal) Nigeria. She recalls her delight when she heard that school children in Zimbabwe were reading her first novel, *Purple Hibiscus* ("The Pleasing Results" 1 2013).

The experience of living outside Nigeria, extensive travel, and education abroad has fostered a broad appreciation of diversity and, more importantly, recognition of cultural similarities that gesture to historical commonality of African-descended peoples. Part of Adichie's 'enlightened' perspective is the ability to engage with difference in positive ways that breaks barriers of *otherness* within racial parameters of the black world. She reiterates: "My experience as an outsider has very much shaped how I look at the world ... But my eyes are still very Nigerian" (Roberts 2013: 1).

At the same time that Adichie espouses a worldview that affirms African and African diaspora affinity, she celebrates her Igbo Nigerian identity. She states unequivocally:

> My position is that I am Pan-African, I am Nigerian, I am Igbo: I am equally all of those things. I am not going to deny one for the other. I am Igbo because my perception of the world was very much colored by being raised by Igbo parents; going to an Igbo village many times a year. I am not a world citizen. I don't know what that is. I have a Nigerian passport; I don't know what a world citizen is.
>
> (Adichie 1)

Adichie poignantly captures the complexities of human experience and shifting perceptions of African identity in her refusal to be "only one thing". She extends the metaphor of the "danger of a single story" beyond one-dimensional representations of the African continent to a (re)imagined African identity of diaspora subjects in the global age. Adichie's reference to the term "world citizen" is a rejoinder that counters the configurations and claims of Afropolitan identities expressed in 2005 by Taiye Selasi in the well-known and oft-quoted article "Bye Bye Babar" in *LIP Magazine*.

Selasi's world is peopled with a new breed of hybrid African, fashioned in the transnational spaces of Europe and America as "citizens or Africans of the world". She captures the upbeat and fluid images of "African young people working and living in cities around the globe, they belong to no single geography, but feel at home in many". They, (read we) are Afropolitans-the newest generation of African emigrants, coming soon or collected already at a law firm/chem lab/ jazz lounge near you" (Selasi 2). Selasi's ideas have weathered stringent critique by many contemporary scholars and writers as reductionist, elitist, and exclusionary, suggesting a new "single-storied" reality of the African diaspora in the twenty-first century. These perceptions successfully capture the realities of a subset of privileged Africans whose education, mobility, and sophistication belie an air of what Susanne Gehrmann calls 'cosmopolitanism with African roots' (2016: 61). Moreover, Chielozona Eze affirms: "the more damning weakness of the term ... is in its exclusivity and elitism" (2014: 240). Much of the critique of Afropolitanism by Eze and other scholars and writers derive from Selasie's descriptions: "You'll know us by our funny blend of London fashion, New York jargon, African ethics, and academic successes. Some of us are ethnic mixes, e.g. Ghanaian and Canadian, Nigerian and Swiss; others merely cultural mutts" (2005: 2). Although Adichie, in her life and fictional works conveys some of the features of Afropolitanism, she distances herself in outspoken allegiance to Igbo ethnicity, Nigeria, and Africa. She divides her time between Nigeria and America, fulfilling Simon Gikandi's reinterpretation of Afropolitanism:

> that has been prompted by the desire to think of African identities as both rooted in specific local geographies but also transcendental of them. To be Afropolitan is to be connected to knowable African communities, languages and states. It is to embrace and celebrate a state of cultural hybridity-to be of African and other worlds at the same time.
>
> (2011: 9)

Gikandi's restatement of Afropolitanism more appropriately captures the realities of shifting transnational identities that traverse geo-spatial boundaries within a fluid arena of African mobility in the global age. For Adichie, and a generation of African diaspora writers and intellectuals, living in both Africa and the West has become a norm and, depending upon political inclinations, Pan-Africanism may offer "an ideology that has political agenda in its quest for solidarity between Africans globally" (Kigotho 2016: 1).

Adichie counters Afropolitanism succinctly: "I'm not Afropolitan. I'm African, happily so ... I'm comfortable in the world, and it's not that unusual. Many Africans are happily African and don't think they need a new term" (Roberts 2013: 1). The articulation of Igboness and Africanity is very healthy and empowering, and sparks a sad recollection of the erasure of African identity among African diaspora peoples caused by the trauma of slavery, and centuries of cultural, and geographical discontinuity. Adichie embraces her Igbo ethnic heritage as a source of empowerment, and strong cultural moorings at the same time that she extends her Pan-African worldview outward to African-descended people within a global arena. Juliette Storr, in her examination of cultural differences in the African diaspora, affirms: "the tension created by the need to be different and the same continues to shape the communication practices among Blacks living in the United States" (2009: 670). Although much has changed from a global perspective, this tension has produced the fractures that continues to frame much of the interactions among diverse groups of Africans in the old and new diaspora. Adichie, in her life and works, has bridged this gap through her literary interrogation and engagement with historically generated racial dynamics in America.

In sum, Chimamanda Ngozi Adichie's *Americanah* reveals her commitment to Pan-African ideology and her carefully nuanced interrogation of race and identity in America. The work engages the complexities of diaspora life and the transformative experiences of mobility and diaspora subjectivity in the global age. Very importantly, Adichie has avoided stereotypical presentation of African Americans to (re)construct a positive image in the African diaspora. Like other writers of her generation, her fiction mirrors the lived reality of shifting identities, and abrasive encounters with both white and black populations abroad. Adichie distances herself from identification with the popular (re) framing of contemporary transnational African identity in repudiation of Afropolitanism. She embraces her Igbo-Nigerian identity even though she inhabits two worlds of racial, historical, and cultural difference, Nigeria and America. Utilizing Christel N. Temple's model of literary Pan-Africanism (2004), *Americanah* emerges as a Pan-Africanist text through multilayered representations of theme, characterization, and plot. Moreover, a salient precept of Pan-Africanism is reconnection to Africa and, at the end of the novel, the protagonist returns to Nigeria as homespace. Adichie boldly deconstructs the tensions between African immigrants and African Americans and contextualizes America's ugly and deeply troubled legacy of slavery and the ways in which it divides Africa and her diaspora. The novel conveys the caveat that, for African immigrants in the West, racialized identities are inescapable. In her novel, and in her life, Adichie's accounts of navigating the convoluted path to comprehension of the historical context of racism, presage the need for re-education and mutual understanding. In her life and works, Adichie uses her voice to challenge the idea that centuries of dispersal

Negotiating identity and Pan-African aesthetics 65

of African people need not predict a future of denial, bias, and mutual rejection that counters a basic tenet of Pan-African solidarity.

Works cited

Adesani, Pius, and Chris Dunton. "Nigeria's Third Generation Writing: Histoiography, and Preliminary Theoretical Considerations". *English in Africa*. Vol. 32. No. 1. 2005. pp. 7–19.

Adichie, Chimamanda Ngozi. *Purple Hibiscus*. Lagos. Farafina. 2004.

——— "Interview: Chimamanda Ngozi Adichie Website" www.cerep.ulg.ac.be/adichie/cnainterview.html. 2005.

——— *Half of a Yellow Sun*. Toronto. Alfred A. Knopf. 2007.

——— *The Thing Around Your Neck*. Toronto. Alfred A. Knopf. 2009.

——— *Americanah*. Toronto. Alfred A. Knopf. 2013.

——— *We Should All Be Feminists*. London. Fourth Estate Publishers. 2015.

——— *Dear Ijeawele, or A Feminist Manifesto in Fifteen Suggestions*. London. Fourth Estate Publishers. 2017.

Adichie, Chimamanda Ngozi, and Michael Ondaatje. "In Conversation: Chimamanda Ngozi Adichie, and Michael Ondaatje". *Brick*. Vol. 79. 2007. pp. 38–48.

Adichie, Chimamanda Ngozi, and Synne Rifbjerg. "Americanah International Author's Stage." May 20. Accessed November 13, 2015. www.youtube.com/watch?v=b8r-dP9NqX8. 2014.

Africa in DC. "The Pleasing Results Chimamanda Ngozi Adichie's Wardrobe Malfunction & Her Thoughts on Race, Pan-Africanism and Gender". *Africa in DC*. https://africaindc.wordpress.com/tag/adichie-pan-africanism/. 2013.

Boston Review. "Race doesn't occur to me". *Boston Review*. www.salon.com/2013/07/14/chimamanda_ngozi_adichie_race_doesnt_occur_to_me_partner/. 2014.

Ajeluorou, Anote. "Adichie Fulfills Dream of a Pan-African Space to Validate African Writers". https://guardian.ng/art/adichie-fulfills-dream-of-a-pan-african-space-to-validate-african-writers/. 2015.

Eze, Chielozona. "Rethinking African Culture and Identity: the Afropolitan Model". *Journal of African Cultural Studies*. Vol. 26. pp. 234–247. http://dx.doi.org/10.1080/13696815.2014.894474. 2014.

Gehrmann, Susanne. "Cosmopolitanism with African Roots. Afropolitanism's Ambivalent Mobility's". *Journal of African Cultural Studies*. Vol. 28. No. 1. pp. 61–72. http://dx.doi.org/10.1080/13696815.2015.1112770. 2016.

Gikandi, Simon. "Foreword on Afropolitanism". *Negotiating Afropolitanism: Essays on Borders and Spaces in Contemporary African Literature and Folklore*. Amsterdam and New York. Rodopi. 2011.

Hassan, Salah. M. "Rethinking Cosmopolitanism: Is 'Afropolitan' the Answer?" www.princeclausfund.org/files/docs/5_PCF_Salah_Hassan_Reflections_120x190mm5DEC12_V. 2012.

JSTOR Daily. "Chimamanda Ngozi Adichie: I Became Black". Interview with Hope Reese. *JSTOR Daily.* https://daily.jstor.org/chimamanda-ngozi-adichie-i-became-black-in-america/. 2018.

Kigotho, Wachira. "Pan-Africans versus Afropolitans-An Identity Crisis". University World News. Africa Edition. Issue No. 172. www.universityworldnews.com/article.php?story=20160429165418809. 2016.

NPR. "*Americanah* Author Explains Learning to be Black in The US". *NPR.* www.npr.org/2014/03/07/286903648/americanah-author-explains-learning-to-be-black-in-the-u-s. 2013.

Nyamnjoh Francis B. and Katleho Shoro. "Language, Mobility, African Writers and Pan-Africanism". *African Communication Research.* Vol. 4. No. 1. 2011. pp. 35–62. fakoamerica.typepad.com/.../nyamnjoh-katleho_scripting-pan-africanism_2011_final.

Odhiambo Tom. "I Owe it All to Achebe". *The Daily Nation.* March 12. www.nation.co.ke/lifestyle/weekend/Chimamanda-I-owe-it-all-to-Chinua-Achebe/1220-2111018-h5f39ez/index.html. 2013.

okayafrica.com. "10 Things We Learned from Chimamanda Ngozi Adichie and Trevor Noah". www.okayafrica.com/.../10-things-chimamanda-ngozi-adichie-trevor-noah-discussion. 2017.

Pahl, Miriam. "Afropolitanism as Critical Consciousness: Chimamanda Ngozi Adichie's and Teju Cole's Internet Presence". *Journal of African Cultural Studies.* Vol. 28. No. 1. 2016. pp. 73–87.

Roberts, Jennifer. "New novel shows that Chimamanda Ngozi Adichie gets the race thing". Interview with Jennifer Roberts/*The Globe and Mail.* www.theglobeandmail.com/arts/books-and-media/new-novel-shows-that-chimamanda-ngozi-adichie-gets-the-race-thing/article12423909/. 2013.

Sackeyfio, Rose. "Black Women's Bodies in a Global Economy: Sex, Lies and Slavery" *At The CrossRoads: Readings of the Postcolonial and the Global in African Literature and Visual Art.* Ed. Ghirmai Negash, Andrea Frohne and Samuel Zadi. Trenton, NJ. Africa World Press. 2014. pp.199–210.

Selasi, Taiye. "Bye-Bye Babar". *The LIP Magazine.* Accessed May 20, 2013. http://thelip.robertsharp.co.uk/?p=76. 2005.

Sterling, Cheryl. "Race Matters: Cosmopolitanism, Afropolitanism, and Pan-Africanism via Edward Wilmont Blyden". *Journal of Pan African Studies.* Vol. 8. No. 1. 2015. pp. 119–130.

Storr, Juliette. "A Thematic Interpretation of Cultural Differences in the African Diaspora". *Journal of Black Studies.* Vol. 39. No. 5. 2009. pp. 665–688.

Temple, Christel N. *Literary Pan-Africanism: History, Contexts, and Criticism.* Durham, NC. Carolina Academic Press. 2004.

5 Reimagining home(land) and mirrors of the past in *Diplomatic Pounds* by Ama Ata Aidoo

Ama Ata Aidoo has broken silence with the publication of her third collection of short stories, *Diplomatic Pounds* (2012), whose female characters traverse the boundaries of African women's identity within diaspora spaces of the twenty-first century. Connecting threads of perplexing behaviors bind the stories through the infusion of paradox, discontinuity, and hybrid identities of the female protagonists. A post-colonial framework of analysis accentuates themes of fragmentation, incongruence and crisis of identity experienced by women torn between London and Ghana in several of the stories. This chapter will examine these elements in *Diplomatic Pounds* and interrogate the women characters' appropriation of behaviors and ideas that simultaneously alienate them from African cultural norms and familial connections to *home* while offering new spaces to contest their subjectivities in Africa and the diaspora. As a mode of critical inquiry, a post-colonial lens will explore problematic behaviors and questionable outcomes of women's disconnection to *self* and to Africa.

The release of *Diplomatic Pounds* in 2012 celebrates the return of Ama Ata Aidoo onto the literary stage of the twenty-first century. In her role as an iconic figure among the first generation of African women writers in the mid-1960s, her latest collection of short stories conveys fresh perspectives and insights into contemporary experiences of African women in transnational space(s). This chapter argues that the stories in *Diplomatic Pounds* are unified through themes of fragmentation and the absence of coherent meaning in the lives of migrant African women. Diasporic subjectivity of the female protagonists illustrates a mosaic of contested identities that evokes similarity to Sissie's 'black-eyed squint' in Aidoo's novel *Our Sister Killjoy*.

In crafting the contemporary stories that explore hybrid identity among female characters in *Diplomatic Pounds,* Ama Ata Aidoo has come full circle from portrayal of women's dilemmas in post-colonial

DOI: 10.4324/9781003219323-6

Ghana in her first collection of stories in *No Sweetness Here* (1995). In contrast to Ghanaian women in the colonial and post-independence era who traverse the boundaries of urban and rural spaces, African immigrant women in the twenty-first century must navigate the challenges of life in Europe and America, and reconcile these realities with Africa as homeland. The stories in *Diplomatic Pounds* foreground women's experiences and vividly capture the complexity of problems they face as racial others in foreign lands. With reference to Aidoo's realistic depiction of Ghanaian women in the post-colonial era in *Our Sister Killjoy* (1977) and *Changes* (1991), Vincent Odamtten notes that "For the Ghanaian woman exposed to a Western-oriented education and ideology that disseminated idealized modes of womanhood at variance with indigenous models, the confusion of identity and purpose becomes all the more problematic" (1994: 10). In the twenty-first century arena of massive migration, globalization, and social flux, contested identities increasingly pervade the lives of Ghanaian and other African women.

The short story genre has moved from the margins of the literary world in relation to the novel in the twenty-first century. A plethora of critical essays, theoretical perspectives and academic engagement has revitalized the literary canon (Rodriguez 2013: 195). These winds of change encompass the African and African diaspora production of literature and among critics and writers, a new focus and renewed energy mirrors the complex changes within in a globalized landscape. Ama Ata Aidoo, along with contemporary African women writers like Chimamanda Ngozi Adichie in her collection, *The Thing Around Your Neck* (2009) and Sefi Atta's *News from Home* (2010), has recentered the African short story from the periphery of neglect to counter the prominence of the novel in the past. Contemporary stories in these new collections are linked through the examination of de-centered and culturally dislocated behaviors that redefine what it means to be an African woman. The female characters' engagement with Africa is thus problematic and disjointed against the landscape of Western spaces they inhabit. In his role as a leading literary critic, Ernest Emenyonu, editor of *African Literature Today*, celebrates the creative artistry and trajectory of the genre with the publication in 2013 of *Writing Africa in Short Story*. This collection of critical essays heralds a new age of literary focus on contemporary short fiction.

From a theoretical standpoint, post-colonial literary theory frames the stories in *Diplomatic Pounds* as a meta-narrative of modern dysphoria for African women émigrés in the twenty-first century. Women who migrate from Africa are thrust into a global arena of shifting identities, displacement, and fragmentation that translate into paradoxical elements of the social, economic, and political landscape. African immigrants portrayed in *Diplomatic Pounds* emerge as dislocated subjects whose relationships to homeland is ruptured and disjointed in ways that parallel their splintered identities. As diaspora subjects, the characters illustrate their inability to reconcile their fractured existence in transnational space(s) with cultural roles and expectations of their families in Africa. These ideas confirm ambiguities and elusive interpretations of what it means to be African. The women in the stories share characteristics of ambiguity, fragmented views of cultural identity, and socially disruptive family relationships.

In most of the stories in *Diplomatic Pounds,* a gendered lens mirrors these elements through hybridity as a focal point of interlocking themes of disquieting reconnections to home, generational conflict, and interracial relationships. Migraine-George contextualizes several decades of Aidoo's creative artistry when she notes that as early as the 1960s and 1970s she "was tackling issues relevant both to the specific conditions of African Literature and to various aesthetic and ideological aspects of literary postmodernity: homelessness, exile, the loss of personal and communal bearings" (2003: 84) in works like *Anowa* (1970) and *Dilemma of a Ghost* (1965). In addition, Haiping Yang highlights the significance of *Our Sister Killjoy* (1977) as "one of the most prominent texts of twentieth century world literatures" (1999: 94) through the penetrating insights into trans-nationality and the creation of "borderland subjects" (94). As a contemporary work, *Diplomatic Pounds* reconfigures the African woman's engagement with diaspora landscapes of hybrid identity.

"New Lessons" is the first story in *Diplomatic Pounds* and examines cleavage and disjointed connections to Ghana as homeland. The unnamed protagonist is a retired college professor who narrates her experience of returning home after years of living in London. When she arrives at the airport, a flashback to her last visit reveals her feeling that with each step she is "getting enveloped into, or swallowed by ... something. Something quite unpleasant and alien. Something like solid air. Thick and clammy. With a sweet unsettling scent. Like clean and perfumed death ... That's it (2012: 2). It is ironic that, for the returnee, 'home' has become a foreign space occupied by her relatives whom she describes as "that amorphous humanity" (2). These unwholesome perceptions are a startling contrast to conventional expectations of warmth, anticipation, and excitement at seeing one's family again after years apart. The irony is twisted further through the narrator's use of metaphorical description that conveys returning home as "perfumed death" and being swallowed by something "unpleasant and alien" (2).

The un-African flavor of her perceptions is antithetical to Ghanaian cultural moorings and family-centered values that nurture cohesive kinship relationships in a communal society.

The strength of African extended families is well documented. Aborampah and Sudarkasa note that "a review of the literature pertaining to families in Africa and wherever the African Diaspora is found, indicates that extended families continue to exist as culturally meaningful units" (2011: 4). Her hybridized identity in London has shifted and reconstructed her cultural center so that, upon return to Ghana as home (space), the environment seems 'alien'. The narrator's repudiation of Ghanaian cultural identity represents a denial of selfhood and signals fragmented identity that is characteristic of postcolonial subjects.

According to Stuart Hall, temporal and spatial differences "produces the postmodern subject, conceptualized as having no fixed, essential or permanent identity" (1996: 598). The feelings of alienation remain even after she is warmly welcomed by her nieces and nephews as they drive away from the airport. The protagonist remarks that "the thing into which she is sinking never went away. Or faded. Or dissolved. Indeed, what was dissolving was me" (2012: 3). For the protagonist, 'me' becomes the rejected African self, permanently altered by living abroad. Thus, life in London is a site of hybridity and diffusion of cultural identity in ways that evokes W.E.B. Dubois' articulation of double-consciousness. She is at 'home' in Ghana and yet her cultural identity is collapsing. The incongruity of 'perfumed death' in her homeland probes the core of the post-colonial dilemma for contemporary African women that live outside Africa.

The spatio-temporal dimensions of the story highlight the tension between the local and global environment, the individual and society, and amplify the loss of cultural moorings for African subjects. Ama Ata Aidoo interrogates the metamorphic landscape of Western spaces that nurture individualistic rhythms in the psyche of African immigrants. The group-centered relationships and bonds of kinship at the core of Ghanaian culture no longer offer a sense of belonging and acceptance. In contrast, the protagonist describes feelings of dread and foreboding, evoking the imagery of a person flaying in a sea of uncertainty. Tanure Ojaide, in "Migration, Globalization and Recent African Literature", notes that in contemporary African literature about African migrants: "the characters that leave Africa for one reason or the other express relief, so do those characters that go back to Africa have initial problems and eventual self-fulfillment. Generally there is a new type of alienation" (2008: 46). In "New Lessons", the protagonist does not experience eventual self-fulfillment and, paradoxically, in a conversation with her favorite niece she acknowledges that she never wanted to live in Ghana anyway. In a reflective moment, she reveals her insistence:

> on staying permanently abroad with infrequent visits home, but my children, her cousins have never ever gone home. Over the years I never managed to make my country seem like an attractive place for either of my two daughters or my son to visit. And as a place to live and work? Forget it. Now, everything is worse down there of course. So much worse than it ever was.
>
> (2012: 3)

Unlike the prevailing convention of African immigrants return home towards the end of their lives, for the protagonist, Ghana can never be a final resting place and she thinks to herself that "at her age, what can she do about anything, beyond returning home like a good old African elephant to die? Actually, I won't even do that ... No, I'm just never going back there" (2012: 4) "New Lessons" has presented a paradoxical and problematic portrait of a Ghanaian woman entangled in a web of identity confusion in a contemporary setting.

The perpetual erosion of cultural identity is an un-settling consequence of the massive globalized movement of people that creates layers of contested realities in post-colonial sites. There are no easy or comfortable solutions to the complexity of social, economic, and political forces that act upon people as social beings. Literature, along with anthropology, psychology, cultural studies, and sociology, explore the relationship of the individual to society and highlight the cohesive nature of collectivist cultures as a generally stabilizing feature of human existence. Extended family networks, responsibilities and kinship ties that are intrinsic to African 'traditional' culture, are very binding, but these are changing in the global arena of migration and displacement. Globalization engenders dramatic changes in people's relationships to home and, in his discussion of the question of identity, Stuart Hall succinctly articulates debates about 'identity' in social theory as follows:

> In essence, the argument is that the old identities that stabilized the social world for so long are in decline, giving rise to new identities and fragmenting the modern individual as a unified subject. This so-called "crisis of identity" is seen as part of a wider process of change which is dislocating the central structures and processes

of modern societies and undermining the frameworks which gave individuals stable anchorage in the social world.

(1996: 596)

Aidoo's commitment to social realism effectively captures these kinds of changes through the behaviors and difficult choices of the women characters in *Diplomatic Pounds*.

The story "Funnyless" is another window into the transnational space that unfolds the post-colonial underpinnings of the collection. The story is told in flashback by Victoria, a retiree who returns to Ghana for the funeral of her mother. She lives in England with her husband and two sons. Similar to "New Lessons", a post-independence framework contextualizes the protagonists' hasty departure from Cape Coast after only one week because of irreconcilable contradictions between life in England and cultural expectations of her family in Ghana. Similar to the unnamed protagonist in "New Lessons", Victoria experiences a break with Ghana as a locus of her cultural belonging that illustrates fragmented self-perceptions. The gradual erosion of familial bonds and responsibilities is displayed through her resistance to needless and exorbitant funeral expenses for her mother's burial. This represents Aidoo's critique of expensive and ostentatious funerals that is pervasive among many contemporary Ghanaian and other African peoples in urban settings. Victoria asks herself, "is this the home she had missed and dreaded to return to in equal measure?" (2012: 128). The characters' hybridized consciousness causes her to replay conversations with her relatives in English. She thinks to herself that "she listened to their language, and also did her simultaneous translation: a habit she has acquired over the years" (129).

The reference to *their* language connotes a splintered consciousness and frames her life as a diaspora subject with the attendant cultural disorientation. Victoria perceives her people as "the other", reminiscent of the "double consciousness" articulated by W.E.B. Dubois in *The Souls of Blackfolk* (1903). Her Ghanaian language is no longer the cultural marker and intrinsic feature of her ethnic identity and sense of belonging to Africa. In her analysis of Tsitsi Tsiti Dangarembga's classic, *Nervous Conditions* (1988) Nfah-Abbenyi and Makuchi examine Nyasha's loss of her indigenous language, Shona as a mark of assimilation and rejection of selfhood. They assert that "language is that which grounds subjects ontologically and epistemologically. Thinking in English demonstrates how disruptive this process of assimilation can be ... Assimilation alienates and negates Nyasha's Shona-self, positioning it as Other while affirming and reinforcing her English-self" (1997: 64). In *Nervous Conditions* Nyasha's crisis of identity is a result of having been torn away from her language at age ten, in contrast to Victoria who is an adult. Language confusion at her age is uncommon among first-generation immigrants who most often retain and prefer to speak their languages, even in the midst of other forms of acculturation and assimilation into Western spaces. In an effort to assert her new diaspora identity, she "catches herself again translating the exchanges into English, inconsequentially, but also as though to escape into that other, and yes safer world" (2012: 130). The idea of escape and safety into transnational space(s) in the West that historically, culturally, politically, and socially identify African people as the 'other' is a perplexing reversal of polarity.

Regardless of the extent to which an African immigrant woman identifies with her country, James Clifford notes that, "diaspora women are caught between ... ambiguous pasts, and futures. They connect and disconnect, forget and remember, in complex strategic ways. The lived experiences of diasporic women thus involve painful difficulty in mediating discrepant worlds" (1994: 314). Similar to the protagonist in "New Lessons", the expressions of affinity to England makes her feel secure and safe, whereas the Ghanaian cultural space evokes feelings of dejected and dysphoric mental states. Aidoo's creative artistry weaves added layers of conflict through infusion of gender preference that fuels Victoria's hasty exit from Ghana with her sons. Her boys are considered the wrong gender among her matrilineal kinship group. She had never brought them home before this visit and, all along, they assumed her children were girls. She is returning to London prematurely after she and her husband planned to resettle at home and start a business. These plans are shattered when the narrator observes that she will get her boys

> away from all those people who seem to think that here too, the boys are somehow not good enough to be considered fully human ... She kept asking herself these and other questions until she concluded that it's some kind of upside down space, the world of those Akans.
> (2012: 130–131)

In a paradoxical twist, Aidoo has skillfully super-imposed gender issues onto the post-modern contentions of the story.

The contraposition of gender preference for female children is heightened when one of Victoria's female relatives asks, "what are we going to do with boys?" (2012: 132). This makes her feel completely "deflated, disgusted and furious" (132). Before leaving she asks herself whether normal people question their societies. It is impossible to reconcile these antagonistic realities in Ghana and she decides to leave abruptly. When she tells her husband she is coming 'home' next week with the boys "he hisses into the phone: Coming back home? But you are home? That last statement hit Victoria so hard it stops her from breathing for a second" (138). Stuart Hall poses the question of whether the world is moving towards the global post-modern. He states that when migrant individuals gradually refer to their new 'space' as *home* one might agree with theorists who argue: "there is evidence of a loosening of strong identifications with the national culture and a strengthening of other cultural ties and allegiances, 'above' and 'below' the level of the nation-state" (1996: 621). At variance with this idea is the continued allegiance to England as 'colonial home' or mother country that many Ghanaians retain in the twenty-first century as part of their history (Aborampah 2011: 98).

Once again, perceptions of 'home' take on a new meaning and it is no longer the site of unconditional acceptance and belonging for many immigrants. The existence of competing identifications and apperceptions may drive a wedge between families and dislocate the centrality of Africa as homeland for immigrant subjects. Aidoo's treatment of gender in both stories suggests that sometimes incongruities arise not from the characters at the center of the story but from those that occupy 'homespace'. Time and distance constrain family ties across transnational boundaries in ways that summate layers of dysfunctionality for post-colonial subjects.

"Diplomatic Pounds" is the cardinal story in the collection, whose salient features contextualize the entire work. The title is a metaphor that translates the *weight* of Western privileged existence into the lives of an elite Ghanaian ambassadorial family. Typical of Adioo's well-documented style that employs wry humor and wit, the story is a colorful rendering of a young woman's obsession with food and weight. The author's selection and treatment of this conspicuous and excessive predilection of the West is a window into the ways in which ideas and behaviors are transmuted among emerging and globalized communities of African immigrant women.

Cecille is the protagonist whose increasing obsession with food and weight portends a dark undertone of the narrative because she 'loses' herself at the end of the story. The setting is London and the narrator is her mother whose maternal perceptions are more than trustworthy as the gatekeeper of sanity and decorum. Cecille's father is a diplomat and the family's privileged existence takes on a new but unfavorable meaning for her through the over-consumption of food. Aidoo has likely chosen food and its abundance as a timeless and universal signifier of well-being and comfort. In weaving the story around consumption of food, the work illustrates the appropriation of inimical and consumptive behaviors as part of diaspora behaviors of African women. In a comical conversation between mother and daughter, Cecille asks "what's the point of being in the diplomatic service if one isn't going to explore the foods of other people?" (2012: 34). Her mother replies that it is not part of her father's mission for his family to "carry the weight of his job on their person" (34).

Cecille's obsession stretches the absurdity as she is said to "own bathroom scales from the early 1920s to tomorrow morning" (2012: 34) as they are scattered liberally throughout the whole house. The comic dimensions of the story belie a serious undertone after mother and daughter consult a European psychiatrist and it is revealed that Cecille has had a nervous breakdown. Her mother has employed a cultural outsider because she fears gossip from the African community. Aidoo skillfully builds the irony as her mother casually remarks that "people don't change because they now live here in London instead of Accra, Lagos, Freetown or Monrovia. In fact, they are worse here. Life is easier, so people have more time to gossip. They'll be whispering that the ambassador's daughter has gone crazy. But Cecille has not gone crazy. She is just having a nervous breakdown" (Aidoo 37). None of the characters experiences an epiphany at the end and, considering the seriousness of Cecille's mental condition, her mother's casual tone and preoccupation with what others will think is disheartening at best. "Diplomatic Pounds" is a satirical story, albeit its dark-themed plot that positions the female characters' within a dynamic interplay of unwholesome behaviors that are far removed from African cultural norms. Cecille's character displays a downward spiral as she moves further away from her cultural center, which might be termed 'a descent into madness'. There is almost nothing Ghanaian about Cecille Wiggleton. Although her character is not described in great detail, her name suggests a shallow imitation of a European woman. Rajendra Kumar Dash aptly describes her puzzling condition "as a situation where the individual sits powerless, without the agency to strive and have a meaningful life" (2013: 236).

If this premise is accepted, Cecille's *idees fixes* in "Diplomatic Pounds" confounds her ability to navigate reality, and as she 'loses' herself to the obsession with food, she no longer recognizes what is *real* around her. For her, the post-independence landscape is a pitfall that does in fact *swallow* her sanity. She is pitiable as she sits powerless and voiceless against the ravages of diaspora subjectivity, trying to be something she is not. The need for acceptance and belonging within antagonistic foreign spaces is a strong influence on women's behaviors. As cultural and racial outsiders, many women feel the need to adopt new behaviors and ideas.

The juxtaposition of African and European aesthetics is the subject of "Mixed Messages", which is another parody of food consciousness coupled with body image among a group of African and African diaspora women. The story traces their episodic encounters over several years through the voice of the narrator, Quaaba. The twenty-first-century compulsion over food is treated differently than in "Diplomatic Pounds". The tension in the story explores mixed messages about food and weight that complicates the women's perceptions of themselves and each other. The women are educated, well-travelled, and sophisticated and, over time, they forge a sisterhood. They are based in New York and meet regularly to share their experiences. The story suggests that African and African diaspora women face the unrelenting challenge to reassert their identities to achieve some form of balance in their lives within a transnational arena. Omar Sougou corroborates the idea of appropriation of non-African images as follows: "African diaspora subjects articulate identities constructed far away from their homelands or motherlands both in fiction and critical theory" (2010: 130). By virtue of their marginalized identity and status in the world, they constantly renegotiate their identities within and among themselves in a world that is hostile to women of color.

Quaaba, the narrator, begins the story in Ghana as a young girl whose culture, by way of her grandmother and other females in her environment, nurtures positive perceptions of her body image. She remembers that:

> as far as her grandmother and her age mates were concerned my butts stood out like the two solid supports they should be: for my backbone, my hips, my thighs, my legs ... Thanks to Nana and everyone else around me when I was growing up, I was convinced that I had the perfect body.
>
> (2012: 144)

She says that her ideal body but imperfect face followed her through her youth. Years later, the contrast to Ghanaian aesthetics and healthy acceptance of her physical appearance vanishes when she leaves Africa. She recounts how:

> From the moment I stepped off the plane in Europe and throughout my many years' sojourn here in North America, it was not my face

that got me into trouble. I have had to squeeze what have turned out to be my unacceptably large bottoms into all manner of corsets and girdles and body shapers. Clearly, out here I am one of the women for whom spandex was invented, while also learning quite early that nothing has ever or will ever re-engineer my body to give me that "dream shape to die for".

(2012: 144)

Throughout the world Caucasian features and European aesthetic ideals have become the standard by which women are measured. Historically, the black female body is cast as over sexualized, objectified, and unacceptable. For many women of color, this reality is a bitter pill to swallow. Quaaba adds that it was the shape of her body that almost drove her into therapy. Though comical in flavor, this colorful anecdote realistically portrays one of many disjointed realities that African women may encounter when they leave Africa. And, although outwardly simple, it represents a mosaic of contested identities and unfavorable self-perceptions. In an interview with Maureen Eke and Vincent Odamtten in 2012, Ama Ata Aidoo explains her inspiration for this story:

I find myself exploring the food in New Orleans against the background of what I call the specific criminalization of obesity in Western – and gradually global – culture. Somebody who is anything from 2 pounds overweight to whatever- is actually regarded as anti-social and almost criminal.

(2012: 165)

As the women meet regularly, Quaaba observes that "getting together was no longer benign ... soon everyone wanted to hurry to the crucial business of our weight" (Aidoo 2012: 151). Eventually, the only thing the women talk about is weight loss, weight gain or diets. Their discussions begin to center on which of them has either lost or gained weight and why. One after the other they rush to weigh themselves when they are together. In a bizarre twist, warped perceptions about body image, unrealistic expectations and stress causes one of the women, Julie, to collapse at a family holiday gathering. The women in her family look like thin fashion models and make her feel afraid to eat. She revolts against the *weight* of the unwholesome emphasis on being thin and the mixed messages in the story are the ambiguous, absurd, and illogical realities of Western and African perceptions of beauty. These uncomfortable perceptions represent another stratum of the post-independence landscape in the twenty-first century. The ways in which women challenge these difficult predicaments is rarely in their best interest and, like Cecille in "Diplomatic Pounds" and Julie in "Mixed Messages", it can lead to dangerous consequences for women. Both characters exhibit neurotic behaviors. The larger conflicts that emerge in both stories is the assault on women's identities as they move beyond their African cultural spaces. Intolerance for diversity, outright discrimination, *otherness*, and marginalized status in diaspora spaces illustrates the conflation of race and gender in a globalized world.

Of all the stories in *Diplomatic Pounds* "Rain" more accurately fits the conventions of the short story in form and structure. Elements of shifting points of view and symbolism are prominent features that extend the post-colonial dimensions of the story through the omniscient narrator's voice. As the longest story in the collection, the narrative strategies create a more satisfying flow of events that connect skillfully to the symbolism of the title. The fleeting encounters, ambiguity and lack of communication shapes a well-crafted story of failed romance of a young Ghanaian woman who has returned home from London. Like the other stories in the collection, the setting includes both London and Ghana and Affiye is a product of both worlds. What is different about this story in comparison to the others explored above is the presentation of more of the protagonists' life in England as a richly textured background that connects to her past, present, and future. As a Ghanaian woman, her good fortune is her sponsorship in London by her well-established uncle and father figure that helps to shape her perceptions of Ghana and her identity in England as an uprooted African.

"Rain" stands out from the other stories through its complexity and intricately constructed interplay of three characters who emerge as post-colonial subjects along with Affiye, the protagonist. The story is a brilliant exposition of modern individuals' dilemmas in a rapidly changing landscape of antagonistic energies. All the characters are swept into a whirlpool of confusion and uncertainty. Affiye, her uncle Appau, and Mathias Koessler form the story's nexus, which shapes the unfolding plot between London and Ghana. Within each character's life, and among each other, the contradictions and problematic perceptions that are displayed forms a subtext of the story's elusive message and perplexing ending. Affiye is trapped in a swirl of anxiety that orbit her life as she traverses Ghanaian and European boundaries as well as crossing racial borders with a German man, affectionately known as 'Matty'. Affiye's life in London and the story as a whole, is colored with incompatible realities that intensify and build within her as a web of ambivalence.

These muddled and puzzling elements of the story are heightened through the jarring and disparate collisions within Affiye's unresolved relationship with Matty, whom she meets at a lecture in London. Aidoo skillfully infuses shifting points of view to illustrate that they come from two different worlds that are not only diametrically opposed, but spell disaster for a sustained romance and marriage in the future. Affiye is reluctant to respond to Matty's growing interest and, when she finally tells him her name, they begin to meet regularly at a retreat. Throughout the story their exchanges are marred by lack of communication, awkward silences, and mixed messages. The narrator parallels each character's indecision and reluctance to fully engage and share their experiences, so that neither Matty's nor Affiye's emotions develop into a lasting commitment. Their feelings are submerged and stifled in ways that clearly foreshadow a failed romance against the background of shifting positionality in time and space.

The most significant event and defining moment in their relationship takes place at a retreat and this meeting is, at best, a fleeting encounter that is laced with symbolism of water as a major subject of their conversation. The narrator observes that, "When they talked, or rather when she talked, it was mostly about the river. How beautiful and cool it was. Quite often she would just talk about water generally, praising its life-giving life-saving qualities properties." (Aidoo 2012: 87). They hardly communicate because Affiye, "never seemed to listen to him and when she did, she never seemed to have heard him. She would ramble on and on about how little water they had at home" (88).

Her references to water are profuse when she describes the distances her mother's people had to walk looking for water, rivers in Europe, and melting snow that turns to water. Her enthusiastic ideas about water appear strange to Matty, and seem like an unsettling obsession so that:

> after a while he began to feel a little uneasy and even apprehensive .... So once in a while, he would try and think of something to say that was not quite a criticism of her, but which he hoped would put a little damper on her enthusiasm. Like reminding her of how voracious and dangerous water can be. 'People drown you know,' he said, with a vehemence that was quite out character.
>
> (2012: 88)

Aidoo introduces elements of foreshadowing through the rather elaborate juxtaposition of water's positive and potentially destructive qualities, which forms a bridge to the story's theme and symbolism of rain. In addition, the author introduces poetic elements to further magnify the metaphorical dimensions of water as follows:

Sailors at work.
Voyagers on business and at play.
Fisherman at sea. Anglers on land.

> We drown in rivers and lakes and ponds.
> Swimming pools and bathtubs.
> Rain storms that kill.

The short story form allows Aidoo the flexibility to experiment with positionality through the meandering and inconsistent patterns of Affiye's and Matty's movements at this meeting that symbolizes the impermanence of their relationship. For example, the narrator describes how they were "crossing the road, going over the small bridge and then turning left of the stream and sitting on an embankment" (86). After the verbal skirmishes over water, Affiye "got up, turned left and crossed the bridge, as though she was going to run 'home' that very minute. So he too stood up, turned left and trotted after her as if to stop her" (2012: 91). When he catches up with her, they sit in silence for a few moments on the embankment. Although physically together, each of them is enveloped in silence. Foreshadowing a sad parting later, Matty thinks to himself that, "he did not understand her, but he was becoming quite nervous about where all her anxiety about water was leading them" (92). The barrier between them is apparent because "somehow they had not found it possible to speak to one another again" (93). This is a turning point in the story where Aidoo repositions their crumbling encounter at the end of the retreat:

> Later, in different worlds and at different times, each of them often revisited the time between that last visit to the river and that morning at breakfast; the retreat breaking up; people getting on different buses depending on where in town they were headed for. And then that fleeting moment when they had each caught each other looking and they had not said a word to one another. They were to wonder separately and endlessly, what could have gotten in to them. The heartbreak that was always like a slow burning fire in her would occasionally flare up and attack her guts, so that she would have to find somewhere very quickly to throw up.
> (2012: 93–94)

The transitory and ephemeral nature of the cultural landscape surrounding Affiye prevents a meaningful understanding of her emotions, and herself as a woman. She is torn between conflicting realities of the multi-local spaces in her life that precludes the possibility of a blossoming romance with a man from another race and culture.

Matty's point of view frames the contradictions in the story as he battles his own demons. His dilemma with Affiye stems from his resistance to racist perceptions about people of color because:

> He had guessed early on that communication between them wasn't going to be easy ... Everything came to them loaded with implications. Everything. The sun, the moon, clothes, music and all other art forms. Food and drink? Definitely. And not just the regular jokes about black coffee, *café au lait* and chocolate. But crazier references to chicken ... you know ... dark meat, light meat.
> (2012: 73)

He is haunted by these kinds of racially charged perceptions from his childhood that he refers to as "messengers from home, from his mother to be specific, to remind him what he'd been told and taught about Africa and Africans. And they stayed with him." (2012: 74).

Affiye's anguished response after parting from Matty conveys inner turmoil but Aidoo quickly shifts the action to her plans to return to Ghana at the insistence of her uncle. Having spent 30 years in England without returning home, Uncle Appau's detached perceptions are puzzling to Affiye. Eventually, she returns home, settles in and assumes a satisfying career. The final scene unravels with utter consternation when, as the pastor asks her to kiss the groom, she sees Matty in the crowd. When their eyes lock, it begins to rain and Affiye "cannot tell whether the water running down her face is her tears or from the rain" (2012: 107). The story ends on an ambiguous note when she starts falling backwards: "It is never going to be clear to anybody or even to herself, whether as she is swaying gently backwards, she is actually passing out or not...In any case, she is never going to remember how this whole incredible afternoon ended" (107). The ending is reminiscent of the feminist classic, "The Story of an Hour" by Kate Chopin (1894) where the unexpected appearance of Mrs Mallard's husband causes her untimely demise.

In any case, the symbolism of water is brought to bear from the earlier poetic line, "Rain storms that kill" (Aidoo 2012: 88). Affiye's occasion for happiness at home in Ghana is brutally shattered by Matty as the symbol of her diaspora disorientation. His reappearance is a representation of the transnational space of their lives that proves uncompromising and disquieting on a psychic level. Her feelings of discontent are lurking beneath the surface and confound her life in the future. The story is a vivid rendering of broken identities and the possibility of successful relationships is threatened by local and global tensions.

Ghanaians and other African nationals living abroad who disconnect from their homeland is a compelling motif that intersect in the stories in *Diplomatic Pounds* as a metanarrative of diaspora angst in the twenty-first century. Aidoo has crafted an array of realistic stories that portray the complexity of educated and successful women redefining their identity as they negotiate antagonistic realities in their lives. Although African women in the stories are recipients of education, economic security, and material rewards in the diaspora, crisis of identity may create uncertain outcomes. Relocating to Western nations represents a space for opportunity and self-actualization. However, transcultural identities are fluid and sometimes irreconcilable with African cultural norms and expectations.

In considering inter-textuality of the stories explored in this chapter, Aidoo profiles women that detach themselves from Ghana as homeland, never to return as in "In New Lessons" and "Funnyless". In "Diplomatic Pounds" and "Mixed Messages" women appropriate narcissistic obsessions of the Western world, and succumb to twenty-first-century "nervous conditions" through severe emotional distress. Interracial relationships that spell disaster are the subject of "Rain", the more conventional work in the collection. As a feature of post-colonial analysis, metanarrative elements emerge in all the women's lives because all of them suffer some form of imbalance and incongruity.

The most significant and cautionary theme in the collection is that women feel 'lost' and alienated when they return home to Ghana. Aidoo does not provide solutions to these problematic outcomes but in foregrounding female characters in *Diplomatic Pounds* she has amplified the well-known and often-quoted requisite of Molara Ogudipe-Leslie for the female writer to "be committed as a writer, as a woman and as a Third World person" (1994: 63). Ama Ata Aidoo has lived up to this commitment throughout her literary career, and *Diplomatic Pounds* suggests a caveat for African women's response to trans-national identity. The stories convey social realism and critical insight into challenges of diaspora subjectivity in the age of global transformation. In revitalizing the short story genre, Aidoo has crafted a vivid portrait of African diaspora life and the uncertainty of preserving African identities.

Works cited

Aidoo, Ama Ata. *The Dilemma of a Ghost*. White Plains, NY. Longman. 1965.
—— *Our Sister Killjoy*. White Plains, NY. Longman. 1977.
—— *Changes, A Love Story*. New York. The Feminist Press. 1991.
—— *No Sweetness Here*. New York. The Feminist Press. 1995.
—— *Diplomatic Pounds & Other Stories*. UK. Ayebia Clarke Publishing. 2012.
Aborampah, Osei-Mensah and Niara Sudarkassa. Introduction. *Extended Families in Africa and the African Diaspora*. Trenton, NJ. Africa World Press. 2011. pp. 1–18.

Adichie, Chimamanda. *The Thing Around Your Neck*. Toronto. Alfred A. Knopf. 2009.

Atta, Sefi. *News from Home*. Northampton. Interlink Books. 2010.

Chopin, Kate. "The Story of an Hour". New York. Vogue Magazine. 1894.

Clifford, James. "Further Inflections Toward Ethnographies of the Future". *Cultural Anthropology*. Vol. 9. No. 3. 1994. pp. 302–338.

Dangaremgba, Tsitsi. *Nervous Conditions*. London. The Women's Press. 1988.

Dash, Rajendra Kumar. "Is Postmodernism Dead? *Language in India*. Vol. 13. No. 4. 2013. pp. 235–246.

Dubois, W.E.B. *The Souls of Black Folk*. New York. Barnes and Noble. 1903.

Emenyonu, Ernest, ed. *Writing Africa in the Short Story: African Literature Today*. London. James Curry. 2013.

Hall, Stuart, et al. *Modernity: An Introduction to Modern Societies*. Oxford. Blackwell Publishers. 1996. pp. 596–632.

Migraine-George, Therese. "Aidoo's Orphaned Ghosts: African Literature and Aesthetic Postmodernity". *Research in African Literature*. Vol. 34. No. 4. 2003. pp. 83–85.

Nfah-Abbenyi, Juliana Makuchi. *Gender in African Women's Writing: Identity, Sexuality and Difference*. Bloomington. Indiana University Press. 1997. pp.35–72.

Odamtten, Vincent, Maureen Eke and Stephanie Newell. Introduction. *The Art of Ama Ata Aidoo: Polylectics and Readings Against Neocolonialism*. Gainsville. University Press of Florida. 1994. pp. 1–13.

———. Interview with Ama Ata Aidoo. *African Literature Today*. Vol. 31. 2012. pp.162–168.

Ogundipe, Leslie Molara. *Re-creating Ourselves: African Women and Critical Transformations*. Trenton, NJ. Africa World Press. 1994. 57–67.

Ojaide, Tanure. "Migration, Globalization, & Recent African Literature". *World Literature Today*. March–April 2008. pp. 43–46.

Rodriguez, Laura M. Review. "Short Story Theories: A Twenty-first Perspective". *Journal of the Spanish Association of Anglo-American Association*. Vol. 35. No. 2. 2013. pp. 195–201.

Sougou, Omar. "Ambivalent Inscriptions: Women, Youth and Diasporic Identity in Buchi Emecheta's Later Fiction". *New Novels in African Literature Today*. Vol. 27. 2010. pp. 13–27.

Yan, Haiping. "Trans-nationality and Its Critique". *Emerging Perspectives on Ama Ata Aidoo*. Trenton, NJ. Africa World Press. 1999. pp. 93–124.

6 Unbecoming dreams, splintered identities, and routes of return in Taiye Selasi's *Ghana Must Go*

Taiye Selasi's debut novel *Ghana Must Go* (2013) illuminates the complexities of transnational experiences in the African diaspora, which spans America, Ghana, and Nigeria. This chapter examines the vividly sketched rendering of multiple perspectives of six family members that are torn between conflicting worlds of difference in the past and the present. The hyphenated lives and splintered dreams of the Sai family wreak emotional havoc, while hybridity and unresolved issues define their reality. The novel highlights the ways in which reconnection to Ghana generates healing from ruptured familial bonds of the past. This chapter will also interrogate the Afropolitan elements of the novel as expressed in transcultural origins and encounters among the Sai family. Scholars and critics of *Ghana Must Go* assert the Afropolitan framing of the work that mirror Selasi's enunciation of the term in the 2005, essay "Bye Bye Babar". Selasi emerges as an important new writer in African women's immigrant fiction, and *Ghana Must Go* tells the African story through a transnational lens, similar to other contemporary works of African diaspora literature.

The novel situates the spatio-temporal dimensions of disrupted dreams of success and belonging in America. The work is divided into three sections, *Gone, Going*, and *Go*, that chronicle the life journeys of the Sai family. Selasi skillfully conveys the ways in which the complications of race, class, and gender shapes the decisions that people make in the effort to survive. As the novel unfolds, each character grapples with the pain and scars of the past, as a route to healing and recharting a clouded future. The title *Ghana Must Go* comes from the Nigerian presidential executive order in 1983 that all undocumented Ghanaian immigrants must return to Ghana or face detention. An estimated 23 million Ghanaians were deported.

The family of Kweku Sai is at the center of the work, whose characters are connected not only through lineage, but through trauma,

DOI: 10.4324/9781003219323-7

and the search for belonging to each other, as well as acceptance into mainstream American society. The author's life is mirrored in the Sai family origins because Kweku Sai is Ghanaian while his wife Fola is Nigerian. Throughout their lives, the children as well as their parents suffer in secret to cope with the challenges they face in the diaspora that surface through the realities of race, class and gender.

Taiye Selasi's fiction contributes to an array of third-generation female writers from Africa whose lives and works share striking similarities. In the twenty-first century, a flourishing assemblage of successful, award-winning and compelling works of immigrant fiction has been published by women writers educated and based in the African diaspora. The creative artistry of contemporary women artists has shifted the trajectory of African literature to focus the complexities of migrant women's image and experiences within transnational spaces. Leading among them is Chimamanda Ngozi Adichie's sprawling epic, *Americanah* (2016), and short story collection *The Thing Around Your Neck* (2009, Chika Unigwe's *On Black Sister's Street* (2009), and Sefi Attah's *A Bit of Difference* (2013). Other engaging works include NoViolet Bulawayo's *We Need New Names* (2016), and *Homegoing* (2016) by Yaa Gyasi. Finally, *Adua* by Igiaba Scego (2015), *The God Child* (2019) by Nana Oforiatta Ayim and, in 2019 Bernadine Evaristo's *Girl, Woman Other* expand the genre through exploration of Afro-European settings.

This exciting and impressive body of works explore diverse themes that arise in African diaspora spaces, such as race and class dynamics, sex trafficking, hybridity, local and global tensions, and relationships to Africa as homeland. All the works engage women characters that experience hybridity, and most of them evolve agency and resilience in shaping their destinies, unlike the portrayal of women in Anglophone African literature produced in the mid-twentieth century by male writers. Well-known stereotypical roles for women include the archetypical mother figure, submissive wife, or prostitute in early works such Achebe's *Things Fall Apart* (1955), Wole Soyinka's *The Lion and the Jewel* (1959), Elechi Amadi's *The Concubine* (1966) or Cyprian Ekwensi's *Jagua Nana* (1961) and *Jagua Nana's Daughter* (1961). Beginning with Emecheta's groundbreaking London novels, *In the Ditch* (1972), *Second Class Citizen* (1974), and *Head Above Water* (1986) in the twentieth century, the authors of African fiction in the global age have animated feminist synergy that redefines the image of women in contemporary literary production. As part of world literature, women's and gender studies, immigrant fiction, and ethnic and diaspora studies, new fictional works cross boundaries of literary history and forge new identities of personhood, autonomy, agency, strength, and mobility for women.

Taiye Selasi has crafted the narrative structure of the novel that spans the past and present of Kweku Sai and his family. The opening section unfolds Kweku's 'undoing', reflections on his past, and his untimely death. His traumatic experiences, victimization, and failure as a parent unwind through fragmented flashbacks and memories of estrangement from his family. As the patriarch of the family, he appears to have 'made it' in America as a high-powered physician at a prestigious medical center in Boston. Sponsored by a full scholarship, he migrated to America to climb the ladder of success, only to experience racially motivated dismissal that ends his career. When a wealthy white patient dies after an appendectomy, Kweku is blamed. although it is not his fault. His only crime is his *blackness* and, unfortunately, he goes bankrupt in the effort to prove wrongful dismissal. Maximillian Feldner succinctly notes that "the American Dream failed him ... laying open the latent structural racism in the United States" (2019: 136).

Painfully, Kweku recalls his career:

> Twenty years exactly from that to this moment, the whole thing erected on the foundation of a dream:...general surgeon without equal, Ghanaian Carson and the rest of it, Boy-child, good at science, Makes Good-and he had. He had seen the thing through, the whole kit and caboodle, the accolades, the piano lessons, the sprawling brick house, the staggering prep school tuition, the calling "Bye!" every morning at quarter past seven in scrubs and white coat.
>
> (Selasi 2013: 73)

He remembers the sacrifices made, but unmeasured in either US dollars or framed diplomas. At Beth Israel, he conceptualizes the medical establishment as the 'machine' that he felt part of and it made him feel empowered. At the height of his success, he remembers that he had "felt so special, even superior, for being there" (2013: 69). When he is fired, "the machine turned against him, charged, swallowed him whole, mashed him up and spat him out of some spout in the back" (69). He is devastated and crippled by this defeat.

Traumatized by racial *otherness*, Kweku's future is lost to the hospital machinery: "nameless, faceless. The monster" (2013: 68). Unable to find employment at another hospital, he cannot face his wife and family, which changes the course of his life unfavorably. To mask his failure and shame, he keeps the firing secret, leaving home each morning pretending to go to work. Still unemployed, he visits the hospital a year later, and is thrown out by the security guards. His son Kehinde witnesses the humiliating experience. Kweku eventually tells his wife he will never come back, thus ending their marriage with no explanation. Sixteen years pass until news of Kweku's death reach his family in America.

A salient theme in African diaspora fiction is remembrance and return to one's homeland, reconnection to cultural moorings, and recovery of the past. Ato Quayson and Girish Daswani affirm "the question of identity – who am I? – is necessarily entangled with that of place" in the diasporic novel (2013: 3). Kweku recovers his roots when he returns to Ghana, builds a house, and remarries a local woman. Recent works by African diaspora writers convey these themes in ways that reveal the complexities in the lives of African immigrants who contemplate going home for diverse reasons. Intertextual elements of diaspora novels are vividly portrayed in works such as Adichie's *Americanah* where, after living in America for many years, Ifemelu returns to Lagos and recovers her Nigerian *self*. She begins a new life but she has acquired traits of a person who has lived abroad, hence the colloquial term 'Americanah'. This is a popular term that denotes a newly fashioned Nigerian who has returned from the USA although she fully embraces her cultural heritage. Ifemelu's boyfriend Obinze does not return voluntarily from London because he is deported to Lagos. His status as an undocumented immigrant illustrates the challenge to survive abroad under adverse conditions, racial discrimination, and abject poverty. Adichie's short story *The Thing Around Your Neck* (2009) depicts a young Nigerian immigrant enmeshed in crushing alienation in America. When she learns of her father's untimely death, she returns to Nigeria. Similarly, in a story called "Imitation" a neglected Nigerian wife in suburban America chooses to return to Nigeria to reclaim her marriage and her identity.

In Sefi Atta's *A Bit of Difference* (2013), Adeola is based in London and is torn between her life there and the role of wife and mother in Nigeria. Eventually she does return home after deep reflection on the hybrid nature of her unsatisfying life in England. Moreover, in Yaa Gyasi's *Homegoing,* Ghanaian-descended characters, Marjorie and Marcus, are children of the diaspora *and* Ghana. They find their way back to Accra and begin the process of healing, memory, self-discovery. Interestingly, Chika Unigwe's *On Black Sisters' Street*, engages magical realism in the portrayal of Sisi, a Nigerian sex worker in Belgium. She is killed because she tries to escape the people who trafficked her to Europe and ruined her life. Her spirit flies back to Lagos to visit her family and to curse the local trafficker who deceived her.

Likewise, Okey Ndibe vividly explores the choice to return to Africa through his unfortunate protagonist in *Foreign* Gods (2014). Ike is a college graduate who has been driving a taxi in New York for 13 years because no one will give him a job. His fault is his skin color and Nigerian accent. He is penniless and, in desperation, he hatches a plan to return to his village to steal an artifact. He hopes the 'God' will fetch a small fortune from an art dealer back in New York.

These works vividly interpret Africa in the diaspora imaginary of those who sojourn in Western spaces. The fictional representation of duality and displacement appears in realistic contexts expressed in diverse diaspora settings. The global age of transformation and flux has created new landscapes of identity beyond Africa's borders. The recurrence of 'return to Africa' in contemporary literature is a twenty-first-century trope that mirrors the real-life challenges of African immigrants in foreign spaces. All the works are linked to *Ghana Must Go* as a unifying theme of the diaspora longing for home.

Each of the members of the Sai family must grapple with relationships to both Ghana and Nigeria to reconcile their past. Kweku's death is a turning point in all their lives and Ghana becomes the focus of the spatio-temporal nexus that shapes their familial bonds to each other as well as to the past. The novel unravels the hidden secrets and insecurities that are amplified by the absence of Kweku in their lives and the challenges of diaspora existence. None of the family members achieve emotional balance and *wholeness* in his absence and it is only after his death, when they return to Ghana for his funeral, that the family is reconnected. In Maximillian Feldner's "Exploring the Limitations of Afropolitanism in *Ghana Must Go*" he succinctly confirms that: "Together with the cracks and fissures that are obvious in the characters' psyches, these conflicts indicate that, despite their outward successes, The characters' experience of diaspora and hybridity is not positive" (2019: 136).

Out of sheer loneliness, Fola also returns to Ghana to begin a new life even before Kweku's death. Her recollection spans 16 years as a single parent of four children. She is forced to make difficult choices to support her family. Left bankrupt, she sells her home and moves into a small apartment. Her twins, Kehinde and Taiwo, are sent to live with her estranged brother in Lagos. Olu, her eldest, goes to boarding school and Sadie remains with her. She inherits a house in Accra and moves there.

Sadly, when her husband deserts the family, Fola has no career to sustain her because, at age 23, Kweku tells her: "One dream's enough for the both of us" (Selasi 2013: 73), which denotes the sacrifice of her own dreams so that Kweku could become a surgeon. Fola had been accepted to law school with a full scholarship but instead

Unbecoming dreams, splintered identities 89

She would follow him to Baltimore and postpone studying law and give birth to their baby with not a penny to their name and sell flowers on the sidewalk and take showers in the kitchen so that one of them could realize his dream.

(Selasi 2013: 73)

As a wife and mother of four children she lived in the shadow of her husband's brilliant career, starting her own business selling flowers. Secrecy clouds her feelings of insecurity as a mother, which leads to the ill-fated decision to send her twins to her half-brother in Lagos. Her children are there for over three years and the separation builds an emotional wall with Fola for many years to come. Painful revelations surface in Ghana where the family assembles for Kweku's funeral. For Fola, and Taiwo, Ghana becomes the site for healing the damaged mother–daughter relationship. The emotional gulf created by physical separation and secrecy is a corrosive influence that smolders under the surface.

Taiwo and Kehinde are Fola's twins, whose childhood bears the scars of mutual trauma in a painful sexual abuse in Nigeria. According to Yoruba myth, twins are called *ibeji* and are spiritually connected. When they are sent to live with their uncle Femi in Lagos, they enter an unwholesome environment for children where they are vulnerable to adult situations and sexual abuse. Femi leads a questionable lifestyle, surrounded by an all-male staff and dubious visitors at all hours. Auntie Nike falsely accuses Taiwo and Kehinde of sexual intimacy and beats them. Every day for a week Kehinde is forced to violate his sister while Femi watches. The children are threatened and forced to keep silent, never speaking of the experience to each other and become estranged for years after returning to America. They are rescued after being discovered:

> at a party and they were made to wear makeup and to walk around smiling at guests, boys and men, Nigerian and South African and white, of all ages. A gay man from Ghana: "I know who you are." They left without luggage in a taxi with the Ghanaian. He put them on a plane to JFK and they came home.

(2013: 289)

Fola senses that something terrible happened to them, but they are silent. Their behavior is abnormal and, clearly, they need therapy. Ghana is a site of healing and Fola is told the sordid story in Accra where the family has gathered for Kweku's funeral. The horrible details tumble out amidst wracked emotion. Taiwo is overwhelmed and collapses into her mother's arms, both women weeping uncontrollably. The mother–daughter bond is renewed as Fola reacts from somewhere deep within:

> She's never before felt what she feels at this moment. Three feelings at war with her breath, for her strength: first her anger at Femi, the pure crystal hatred, a rage undiluted by pity or doubt; then the grief that is Taiwo's, her shame and her sorrow, a well of it rushing beneath the right breast; then her own shame and sorrow, to know what has happened, to know what she's sensed all along in her twins *who got hurt,* she thinks, *badly, because they didn't have their mother.*
> (2013: 290)

Kehinde suffers in silence as well and is also emotionally damaged. His saving grace is his artistic talent and, despite the depth of his trauma, he is a famous artist who travels the world, which confirms his transnational mobility. Like Taiwo, he is haunted by the past because he has never healed, causing him to attempt suicide. Although successful, his guilt over his relationship with Taiwo in Lagos has never been resolved. Taiwo has been involved with the married dean of her law school, which causes a public scandal in the media. Before departing for Ghana, she and Kehinde fight bitterly when he calls her a whore. This dredges up the sexual encounters in Lagos when they were younger. The siblings have difficult relationships that spell the need for therapy for them all.

Sadie is the youngest of the Sais and her problems arise from identity confusion in the predominately white environment in Boston. Her best friend is a Caucasian roommate called Philae whom she emulates. Hybridity shapes her coming of age and Taiwo "mocks her for speaking like Philae-overusing *whatever* and *like,* or for dressing like Philae … she's never had many African American friends, neither at Milton or at Yale … She admits to herself that she wants to *be* Philae … larger than life" (2013: 145–146). They are inseparable and, because her friend is wealthy, and visible in the media, Sadie clings to their family. To Sadie, the Negroponte's are:

> weightless, the Sais, scattered fivesome, without gravity, completely unbound. With nothing as heavy as money beneath them, all pulling them down to the same piece of earth, a vertical axis, nor roots spreading out underneath them, with no living grandparents, no history, a horizontal – they've floated, have scattered, drifting outward, or inward, barely noticing when someone has slipped off the grid.
> (2013: 146–147)

Like all the members of her family Sadie's emotions are ambivalent. And like the others, she carries buried thoughts of feeling unconnected, which explains her obsession with Philae, and she prefers to spend holidays in her home.

In an argument with her mother, she says "I want to spend Christmas with a *family*" and at 19 she wants to live her life (2013: 156). Sadie returns to school and she and her mother are estranged until they meet in Ghana. The significance of returning to Ghana is underscored not only through physical proximity but also by sharing emotional space and loosening the barriers of silence.

Olu is the eldest son, who shares Sadie's unhappiness about her family's socio-economic status, family discord, and *otherness* in America. Unfortunately, he thinks of his home and neighborhood with disdain and notes the "grayness all around him" (2013: 221). He attends an exclusive school in an upscale neighborhood and notes the sharp contrast in his life. He wonders: "*Why do we live here*...suddenly angry, in *grayness*, like shadows, like things made of ash, with their frail dreams of wealth overwhelmed by faint dread" (221). He admits that he hates the "school bus that ferried him in, like an immigrant, a foreigner, a native to brilliance but stranger to privilege, bused in, then sent home" (221). Olu's acute sense of displacement is unspoken to anyone and, like the other family members, he has no sense of grounding, or comprehension of the larger forces at work in his life as an African in the diaspora. Moreover, his sense of unbelonging is heightened when he feels diminished in the family and jealous of his younger brother Kehinde.

Olu's predicament is linked to Aunty Uju and her son in Dike in Adichie's *Americanah* (2013). Like Olu and his siblings, Dike comes of age to the emotional and psychological challenges of hybridity. He experiences deep confusion, with little sense of African cultural identity, or his past in Nigeria. Dike's feelings of *otherness* are so intense until he attempts suicide. Adichie draws attention to the importance of parental guidance of the children of immigrants in Western spaces. *Americanah* addresses the lurking dangers in families where immigrant parents are so absorbed in achieving the American dream that they neglect the emotional health of their children.

The pursuit of advanced professional degrees can be disruptive of strong family bonds and a nurturing environment for immigrant youth. Unlike Aunty Uju, who is struggling economically, the Sai children are privileged, and well educated. Although Kehinde is the only one who attempts suicide, all the Sai children are emotionally broken in some way, never coming to terms with the absence of their father, or the sexual abuse of Kehinde and Taiwo as adolescents. Sefi Atta explores this theme in her novella *News from Home*. A Nigerian couple, the Daregos, are both medical doctors and parents of two children. Their demanding careers prevent them from spending adequate time with their children, who are growing up *Americanized*. They have developed problematic stereotypes of Africa and make disparaging remarks that mimic Western media stereotypes. The behaviors of immigrant children portrayed in these works are clearly diverse, but the underlying problems of African families – such as hybrid identity, disconnection to Africa, and psychological and emotional health – underscores an important message in *Ghana Must Go*.

While in Ghana, for Kweku's funeral, Olu recalls an earlier visit to his father that was very unpleasant. Kweku has forgotten that three of his children are graduating. Olu decides not to attend his ceremony at Yale but to see his father instead. The experience is unrewarding, unsettling, and painful. His disappointment in Kweku plunges to new depths because he is basically a shadow of his former self, living poorly, arousing pity and shame in his son. Kweku's demeanor conveys defeat and total failure as a father.

Olu has always sought a connection to his roots and is puzzled that the Sai family has no coherent history of their lineage. When visiting friends in Boston, he looks longingly at family photos that display family history. He tells his father: "A legitimate family would have photos on the staircase. At the very least, grandparents whose first names he knew" (Selasi 2013: 251). Olu hated the man Kweku has become and, after ten minutes, he rushes out, straight to the airport and back to America. These are Olu's last recollections of his father, etched in memories of the severed relationship that is never repaired. Olu follows in his father's footsteps to become a successful physician, but the jagged edges of his emotions are constantly at work.

The Sai family comes together in Ghana and the dysfunctional relationships, buried trauma, and smoldering emotions form the undercurrent of the gathering. Fola decides that Kweku's remains should be cremated. His ashes are contained in an urn and on the beach, instead of scattering his remains, Fola thinks "The idea of him scattered seems wrong in some way. We've been scattered enough ..." (2013: 314). To keep Kweku *whole* she places the urn in the water and it floats out to sea. The family is reunited, as funerals everywhere have a way of drawing loved ones, no matter how distant, back into the fold.

As an Afropolitan herself, Selasi conveys deep insight into transnational landscapes that derives from her background as the child of a Nigerian mother and Ghanaian father. She was born in London and raised in Massachusetts, educated in the UK and the USA. Multi-local origins sharpen her perspective on the richness of multi-ethnic heritage across linguistic, ethnic, and geographical settings. She is indeed an offspring of the African diaspora, conveyed so eloquently in her groundbreaking essay "Bye Bye Babar" (2005), ("Or: What is an Afropolitan") published in *LIP Magazine*.

In this essay, she defines *Afropolitanism* lifestyles in glowing terms that project the experiences of successful immigrants who are "African young people working and living in cities around the globe, they belong to no single geography, but feel at home in many. They, [read we] are Afropolitans-the newest generation of African emigrants, coming soon or collected already at a law firm/chemlab/jazz lounge near you" (2005: 2). Selasi says of Afropolitans: "you'll know us by our funny blend of London fashion, New York jargon, African ethics and academic successes (2).

Although criticized by many writers and scholars as elitist and essentialist, the term caught fire as the subject of robust and controversial debate and scholarship across the humanities and social sciences by prominent figures. Simon Gikandi largely supports the salient features of *Afropolitanism* in the foreword to *Negotiating Afropolitanism: Essays on Borders and Spaces in Contemporary Literature and Folklore* (2011). However he acknowledges the "negative consequences of transnationalism, the displacement of Africans abroad, the difficulties they face as they try to overcome their alterity in alien landscapes, and the deep cultural anxieties that often make diasporas sites of cultural fundamentalism and ethnic chauvinism" (11). Further, Salah Hassan, in "Rethinking Cosmopolitanism: Is Afropolitanism the Answer?", evokes:

> Tragic images of African youth, men and women who have perished trekking through the deserts of North African countries in transit to Europe, and of thousands of others who have drowned, (sometimes deliberately left to face such a tragic destiny) while journeying on makeshift boats across the Mediterranean Sea to Europe. Those who have made it alive have encountered a new fortress of draconian laws in a continent that has devoted its energies and legislation to its security-read curbing immigration as felt on a daily basis by Africans living in Europe or the USA.
>
> (2012: 4)

Nigerian scholar and critic, Chielozona Eze, affirms: "the more damning weakness of the term …is in its exclusivity and elitism" (2014: 234–237). Leading writer Chimamanda Ngozi Adichie speaks in opposition to

Selasi's framing of Afropolitanism: "I'm not Afropolitan. I'm African, happily so ... I'm comfortable in the world, and it's not that unusual. Many Africans are happily African and don't think they need a new term" (2013). Despite criticism by these and other scholars and writers, the term enjoys popularity and is useful as a lens to interpret the African presence in transnational spaces of the West.

The greatest contribution of Selasi's coinage of the term is the exultance of globally savvy communities of African immigrants who are successful and highly educated. The celebration of a vibrant and robust African diaspora that struts cosmopolitan lifestyles, global mobility, and fluidity across national, geographical, and linguistic boundaries is indeed a new way of being African in the twenty-first-century world. Further, Afropolitanism disrupts the standard tropes of African victimhood, the abject immigrant, and marginalized demographic of needy migrants who are refugees, asylum seekers, and undocumented aliens in foreign lands. Thus, Afropolitanism embraces a reimagined sense of identity, founded on the lived reality of successful populations of "model African" immigrant communities in America, which is documented in the social science literature, such as John Arthur's *African Diaspora Identities: Negotiating Culture in Transnational Migration* (2010). In 2016, Selasi expressed her sentiments about "Bye Bye Babar", where she conveys her original intention to simply "create a space" (290). Ede interprets the space created by Selasi's Afropolitanism as essentially: "a metropolitan construct of self representation and black agency…" (2016: 89). More appropriately, the term may be defined as "cosmopolitanism with African roots" (Gehrmann 2016). Mukoma wa Ngugi prefers "rooted Transnationalism" because "one has to be mindful that there are many ways of being transnational and rooted" (2018: 182).

The Afropolitan perspective is relevant in *Ghana Must Go* through the hybrid nature of a family whose socioeconomic mobility and high achievements represent the American dream in no small measure. The family exhibits many features of Afropolitanism, but its viability as a framework must be qualified overall. As a whole, the structure of the novel's multi-local settings between Ghana, Nigeria, and America is certainly Afropolitan in flavor and substance. However, the term fails to neatly account for the unfavorable outcomes, fractured dreams and flawed perceptions of identity among the Sai family.

First, none of the family members feels at home in the world or, rather, the multi-local spaces they inhabit. Feldner confirms that: "they feel lost, unbound, and unconnected to any group or history, a lack that is only resolved during a trip to the father's birthplace in Ghana" (2019: 133). Against the backdrop of the American diaspora landscape, the contested identities, ambiguities, and discord of the family mars their happiness. Although they are highly educated, with the privilege to traverse national borders, America and the ensuing hybridity seem to bring out the worst in the characters, playing upon their insecurities, which push them inward and apart from each other. Kweku's failed American dream depletes his agency as a paternal figure. Despite his belief that his Ghanaian wife is a bridge to the past, he can never repair the rupture in any meaningful way.

Fola's potential as a successful professional is smothered by motherhood when she channels her energy to support her husband's dream as *enough* for them both. These elements highlight the gendered realities of African immigrant identities through women's subjectivity in the diaspora. Olu does not fare any better because the feelings of rootlessness and the absence of family traditions haunt him despite his success as a physician. When he visits Ghana, it is foreign to him, and parallels his rejection of his father for his failure. The absence of lineage history unsettles Sadie as well as she admires and seeks acceptance and belonging by emulating her white friend at school. Taiwo withdraws from law school after a scandalous affair and is estranged from Kehinde, who is fighting his own demons.

In sum, *Ghana Must Go* is a glimpse into the hybrid world of the Sai family within transnational spaces in America, Ghana, and Nigeria. Narrated from multi-vocal perspectives, the characters speak with one voice on the ravages of diaspora life in the past and the present. In the search for stable family traditions, connection to roots, and belonging in America, the characters unravel their fractured identities and emotional angst. The spatio-temporal elements in the work trace the family's dismemberment, but the novel comes full circle in Ghana, where they gather for Kweku's funeral. As a site of healing, most of the buried secrets and past trauma are resolved.

Through revelation, reflection, and new perspectives on their lives, family members chart new paths to the future. This suggests that, for African immigrants, return to one's origins is a route toward healing. These ideas invoke the famed Ghanaian symbol *Sankofa*, which expresses the wisdom of return and recovery of one's past as a foundation for the future. For the Sais, 'return' to Ghana is certainly not a panacea for their problems but serves as a new beginning for the troubled family. Notions of 'return' also suggest that, for African immigrants, the complexities of hybridized identity may be addressed through experiencing one's homeland in ways that reawaken cultural identity.

Ghana Must Go gestures to Afropolitan virtues and, at first glance, the work presents the unbound success and fluid identities of characters across multiple landscapes of the African diaspora. For the Sai family, education, privilege, and upward mobility are clearly the features of Afropolitan lifestyles. However, the dichotonic nature of their sojourn in America spells racialized and splintered realities of otherness. The effort to cope with loss, painful experiences, and insecurities in the family is made worse in the absence of a nurturing environment as the soil for healing. These ideas reconfigure the centrality of 'homeland' as a salient theme in African literature in the past and present. From a diaspora perspective, African diaspora writers like Taiye Selasi interrogate return to African origins as a place of refuge, reflection, and healing. Finally, Ghana creates a space for the Sai family to achieve continuity and strength in the landscape of the future.

Works cited

Achebe, Chinua. *Things Fall Apart*. London. Hienemann. 1955.
Adichie, Chimamanda Ngozi. *The Thing Around Your Neck*. Canada. Alfred Knopf. 2009.
——— *Americanah*. Toronto. Alfred A. Knopf. 2013.
Amadi, Elechi. *The Concubine*. London. Heinemann. 1966.
Arthur, John. *African Diaspora Identities: Negotiating Culture in Transnational Migration*. Lanham, MD. Lexington. 2010.
Atta, Sefi. *News from Home*. Northampton. Interlink Books. 2010.
——— *A Bit of Difference*. Northampton. Interlink Books. 2013.
Ayim, Nana Offoriatta. *The God Child*. Oxford, New York, New Delhi. Bloomsbury. 2019
Bulawayo, NoViolet. *We Need New Names*. Bulawayo, New York. Regan Arthur Books. 2013.
Ede, Amatoritsero. "The Politics of Afropolitanism". *Journal of African Cultural Studies*. Vol. 28. No. 1. 2016. pp. 88-100.
Ekwensi, Cyprian. *Jagua Nana*. London. Heinemann. 1961.
———. *Jagua Nana's Daughter*. London. Heinemann. 1966.
Emecheta, Buchi. *In the Ditch*. London. Heinemann 1972.
——— _*Second Class Citizen*. New York. George Braziller 1974.
——— _*Head Above Water*. London. Fontara. 1986.
Evaristo, Bernadine. *Girl, Woman, Other*. New York. Grove Press. 2019.
Eze, Chielozona. "Rethinking African Culture and Identity: the Afropolitan Model". *Journal of African Cultural Studies*. Vol. 26. 2014. pp. 234–247. http://dx.doi.org/10.1080/13696815.2014.894474.
Feldner, Maximillian. "Exploring the Limitations of Afropolitanism in Ghana Must Go". *Narrating the New African Diaspora: twenty-first Century Nigerian Literature in Context*. Austen, TX. Palgrave Macmillan. 2019. pp. 127–145.
Gehrmann, Susanne. "Cosmopolitanism with African Roots. Afropolitanism's Ambivalent Mobilities". *Journal of African Cultural Studies*. Vol. 28. No. 1. 2016. pp. 61–72. http://dx.doi.org/10.1080/13696815.2015.1112770 2016.

Gikandi, Simon. "Foreword on Afropolitanism". *Negotiating Afropolitanism: Essays on Borders and Spaces in Contemporary African Literature and Folklore*. Ed. Jennifer Warwrzinek and J.K.S. Makokha. Amsterdam. Rodopi. 2011. pp. 9–11.

Gyasi, Yaa. *Homegoing, a Novel*. New York. Vintage Books. 2017.

Hassan, Salah. M. "Rethinking Cosmopolitanism: Is 'Afropolitan' the Answer?" www.yumpu.com/en/document/read/34342036/afropolitan-the-answer-salah-m-hassan-reflections-2012-5-.

Membembe, Achille and Sarah Balakrishnan. "Pan-African Legacies" Afropolitan Futures". *Transition*. No. 120. 2016. pp. 28–37.

Nidibe, Oke. *Foreign Gods Inc*. New York. Soho Press. 2014.

Quayson, Ato and Girish Daswani. "Introduction". A Companion to Diaspora and *Transnationalism*. Ed. Quayson, Ato and Girish Daswani. New York. Blackwell. 2013. p. 3.

Roberts, Jennifer. "New novel shows that Chimamanda Ngozi Adichie gets the race thing". Interview with Jennifer Roberts/*The Globe and Mail*. www.theglobeandmail.com/arts/books-and-media/new-novel-shows-that-chimamanda-ngozi-adichie-gets-the-race-thing/article12423909/. 2013.

Scego, Igiaba. *Adua*. Translated by Jamie Richards. New York. New Vessel Press. 2015.

Selasi, Taiye. "Bye-Bye Babar". *LIP Magazine*, 2005. http://thelip.robertsharp.co.uk/?p=76.

―――― *Ghana Must Go*. New York. Penguin Press. 2013.

Soyinka, Wole. *The Lion and the Jewel*. London. Oxford University Press. 1962.

Unigwe, Chika. *On Black Sisters' Street*. London. Jonathan Cape. 2009.

Wa Ngugi, Mukoma. *The Rise of the African Novel*. Ann Arbor. University of Michigan Press. 2018.

7 Transnational gaze(ing) and shifting identities in the short fiction of Sefi Atta and Chimamanda Ngozi Adichie

The short story genre is a fictional landscape to engage the complexities of hybridized existence in the lives of African women. This chapter uncovers the layered realities of alienated African women who navigate otherness and marginalization in transnational settings of Europe and America. The Nigerian female protagonists in Sefi Atta's "A Temporary Position" and "News from Home", and "Monday of Last Week" by Chimamanda Ngozi Adichie, experience hyphenated identities in the space between sites of racial difference in the West. All the stories engage the inner journeys of women, the challenges they face as immigrants, and the shifting and competing realities they embrace as trans-local subjects in London and America. Diaspora perspectives of the characters invoke deep reflection on how to navigate African sensibilities within unwelcoming environments abroad. Jyothirmai and Ramesh confirm, "The renegotiation however is a process fraught with discomfort and marginality but at the same time it endows a position of strength to comment on both worlds" (2015: 56). The transnational 'gaze' of the Nigerian female immigrants is the focus of this examination of short fiction by Adichie and Atta. The fictional works are emblematic of the authors' concern with representations of Nigeria while abroad as well as the issues of migration into Western settings.

It is no surprise that the African short story is gaining attention and merit in the African literary world at pace with the rise of the African novel in the global age. Similar to the (re)imagined post-colonial African novel since the turn of the century, literary production of short fiction is forging new spaces of inquiry into transcontinental settings of the African diaspora. Like the novel, short fiction by African women writers is a reflection of global forces marked by massive social, economic, and political transformation and, very significantly, increasing patterns of mobility that inform the reconfiguration of African immigrant identities. Noted writer and critic Helon Habila asserts the freedom of

DOI: 10.4324/9781003219323-8

African writers to explore a broad range of twenty-first-century themes, and in his vision for the future of African writing he imagines, "a new wave of diasporic African literature as providing a new possibility, a way forward in African literature in general. A way out of the endless loop of nationalism and anti-colonialism" (2019: 159).

In 2013, *African Literature Today* published a special issue called *Writing Africa in the Short Story* and in the editorial essay, Ernest Emenyonu confirms that:

> The younger generation of African writers, in particular, have used the short story to comment on various aspects of life in modern African societies: the senselessness of violence, war, religious bigotry, racism, corruption and all forms of injustice meted to any human group especially women and the disenfranchised 'others' in Africa as anywhere else in the world.
>
> (2013: 6)

Further, interrogation of the post-independence landscape forms a literary bridge from African fiction crafted by first-generation writers whose literature engaged post-colonial themes that are recast or (re) imagined in the global age by a new crop of writers.

In the twenty-first century, the transnational gaze from immigrants, including the authors living in the contemporary African diaspora, is a window into the unfulfilled dreams and uncertain trajectories of the modern nation state. These perceptions are echoed in both novels and short fiction of leading women writers from Africa such as Chimamanda Ngozi Adichie in her collection, *The Thing Around Your Neck* (2009) and in Sefi Atta's *News from Home* (2010). The works of both authors represent a growing body of diaspora fiction that extend post-colonial themes of the twentieth century. New works interrogate compelling and transformative issues in the global landscape that give rise to new challenges in life. In *Narrating the New African Diaspora: twenty-first Literature in Context*, Maximillian Feldner aptly notes that "Nigerian diaspora literature is therefore positioned in a field of tension whose outer poles can be described as transnational/transcultural hybridity and national identity" (2019: 2).

Moreover, short fiction by Adichie and Atta is linked to Ghanaian icon Ama Ata Aidoo, who published an early and classic rendering of postcolonial short fiction called *No Sweetness Here* (1970), followed by *The Girl Who Can and Other Stories in* 1997 and *Diplomatic Pounds* in 2012. This last collection shares intertextual elements with the works of Adichie and Atta, because Aidoo's female characters are immigrants who are disconnected from their homeland of Ghana. Nigerian writer

Akachi Adimora Ezeigbo's literary works includes five volumes of short stories: *Rhythm of Life* (1992), *Echoes in the Mind* (1994), *Rituals and Departures* (1996), *Fractures and Fragments* (2006) and *Magic Breast Bags* (2019).

As one of Nigeria's most accomplished writers, her works bring to center stage the experiences of women in society although her stories are set in Nigeria. In 2020, Afro-British writer, Bernadine Evaristo won the coveted Man Booker Prize for her collection of diaspora short fiction, *Girl, Woman Other* (2019). Celebrated author, Chika Unigwe, winner of the 2012 Soyinka Prize for *On Black Sisters' Street* (2009) published *Better Never Than Late* (2019), as her first collection of short fiction about the Nigerian diaspora in Belgium.

Diverse themes that emerge in these stories are issues of return to Africa, navigating hybridity and racial otherness, gender dynamics, and coming of age, which are prominent among a host of recurring themes that women writers examine. In "Diaspora Identities in Short Fiction by Chimamanda Ngozi Adichie and Sefi Atta" Sackeyfio asserts the idea that "women's identities take on new dimensions in western environments that command interrogation of the African self" (2013: 103). Interlocking themes of race, class, and gender foreground female experiences as expressions of agency, evolving feminist consciousness and self-realization. Although novels will always remain in the forefront of African literary production, the development of short fiction by women compliments the array of works that chronicle diaspora landscapes in the global age.

Sefi Atta's "A Temporary Position" metaphorically captures the flavor of liminality in the experience of a young Nigerian immigrant in London. The story unfolds the ways in which the female protagonist navigates her life as an accountant in a London company. Her uncertain status in what she refers to as a "temporary position" is the focus of the narrative, vividly narrated through a post-colonial lens. An important feature in the works of contemporary women writers is the portrayal of tensions between local and global realities as well as their effect on the lives of women characters. The search for education and economic opportunities that are not available or problematic in Africa is an underlying element in fictional works about African migration in the post-colonial landscape.

In the story, the unnamed female is privileged because of her parents' wealth, as well as her degree from the London School of Economics. Her background provides opportunities, mobility, and the freedom to pursue her success and material comfort. She admits to being one of many educated Nigerians living in London. She recalls that, while some Nigerian immigrants are supported by their parents, others are working illegally in the UK. This represents a twist in the immigrant saga because it is frequently assumed that undocumented immigrants are uneducated and lacking in skills.

The work takes place during the 1990s and the transnational perspective of the protagonist is laced throughout the story through vivid flashbacks of the Nigerian environment that pushed her to migrate to London:

> Everyday in Lagos was defective ... The normal routine was chaos: no light, no water and no use complaining. We'd had three military coups in seven years; one of them had failed. Our latest dictator was calling himself president of Nigeria and our constitution was not yet inn place.
>
> (2010a: 105)

Political instability and economic malaise define this period in Nigeria's history and frequently women endure adversity or unemployment, even when they are educated.

Atta explores these themes in her novels, *Everything Good Will Come* (2005) and *Swallow* (2010c), which feature Nigerian women struggling in the challenging Nigerian environment. In "Recasting Sisterhood and its Ambiguities", Sackeyfio notes that both novels are "laced with images of a diseased political entity that pervades women's lives while clouding the outlook for a future of productivity and economic stability" (2015: 42).

Spatio-temporality marks the constantly shifting perspectives of the unnamed protagonist who contrasts Lagos and London. She sees no future for herself if she remains in Nigeria, despite her privileged status. Her father urges her to come home and start afresh while complaining that her cadre of young Nigerians is essentially shallow because they expect everything in life to be fast and easy. She recalls Nigeria's uneven post-colonial history during which her father's generation came of age as recipients of neo-colonial male privilege as the route to success. She indicts Nigeria's leaders for the recession that occurred after her country's oil boom and the subsequent structural adjustment that ravaged the nation's economy. In stark contrast to her father, her generation faced an uncertain future, with women at the bottom of the economic ladder.

She tells her father: "With the salary I'd earned at the Stock Exchange I had three choices: live with my parents, live in a hovel, or find a sugar daddy. Of course I chose to return to London" (2010a: 106). The protagonists' choice leads to further uncertainty, pretense, and hybrid existence as a temporary receptionist of a company in London.

Working illegally, she is part of a huge community of Nigerian graduates who live double lives by using fake national insurance numbers, receiving financial support from parents, or accepting government assistance. She recalls feeling "glad my home address could pass for a council's flat, and even though my name and features betrayed me, I did not reveal that I was a Nigerian" (2010a: 101). Atta, like many African immigrant writers, narrates the use of fake English accents: "phonetics as we Nigerians would call it" (2010a: 101) to ease the experiences of "otherness" in Western spaces. In a comical encounter after someone discovers she is Nigerian, she distances herself from her country when questioned: "It's not like I've been back there in a while. I really don't identify. I was quite young when we left" (102). Employment as a receptionist unfolds the larger dimensions of the shifting identity of the protagonist, and in the effort to survive she is always pretending and masking her feelings. In only a few weeks she admits boredom: "It wasn't just the job that bored me; it was the whole experience of working in London, the whole one. I couldn't explain" (105). In highlighting her *in-between* status, local and global tensions are heightened when, during an international call to her father in Nigeria, she tells him: "It's rubbish here ... I don't think I can survive more than three years of working in this place" (107). She is unable to reconcile the experience of navigating disparate realities of Nigeria and London. Working in a 'temporary position' is thus a metaphor of her marginalized status among the pretentious behaviors and plastic people in her workplace. She is haunted by her Nigerian identity after learning that a group of Nigerian graduates are arrested for fraud. Again, local and global realities take center stage, made worse when a Nigerian lawyer remarks to the media:

> It's a legacy of the corruption in our governments. For years, government officials have enriched themselves unlawfully and they are never held accountable. The result is that Nigerians don't consider it wrong to steal public funds, and internationally, we're gaining a reputation for fraud.
>
> (115)

The news story causes deep reflection and she later admits feeling sullied, as she wonders: "Where had I learned that it was all right to break laws? Probably from my father ... because he could not have bought a flat in Pimlico on his miserable government salary" (117).

Ironically, she decides to continue working as a receptionist, despite her fear, and the fact that her employers know she is an educated Nigerian. Although her work is distasteful, and boring, she promises to meet her professional responsibilities. The protagonist is enmeshed in the paradoxical world of *difference* that signal her identity confusion, and acceptance of her employment as much more than a 'temporary condition' of hybridity in her life. The post-colonial landscape in Nigeria is a catalyst for misplaced immigrant journeys into transnational spaces of the West. By the end of the story, the protagonist comes to terms with the ways in which educated and privileged Nigerians may embrace the unproductive legacies of Nigeria's failed hopes of a viable nation in the post-independence era. The transnational gaze is thus a site for introspection to unravel hypocrisy in the experiences of Nigerians in the spatio-temporal nexus of the African diaspora.

"News from Home" (2010b) is the centerpiece of Atta's collection, which appropriately shares the same name. Of all the selections in the volume, it embodies the transcultural perspective through extensive development as a novella. Similar to "A Temporary Position", "News from Home" interrogates the contradictions of post-independence through one of Nigeria's most destructive problems, environmental exploitation and degradation in the oil-rich Niger Delta region by the multinational oil industry. The view of Nigeria from America is sharp and clear, as these perceptions raise issues of feminist energy and resilience among women who are struggling to survive.

Sefi Atta's artistry unveils the complexities of the Nigerian immigrant experience for women who must negotiate new identities in the global arena. For the women in "News from Home", the perceptions of Nigeria from abroad are a way of contextualizing the past, present, and future for themselves as global actors in the twenty-first century. Carole Boyce-Davies notes the shifting spaces of identity for migrant females: "The re-negotiating of identities is fundamental to migration as it is fundamental to Black women's writing in cross-cultural contexts" (1994: 3). Adichie and Atta craft fiction that mirror these modalities in their woman-centered fiction.

The multi-local settings of "News from Home" include Nigeria's Niger Delta, and New Jersey, where Eve awakens to a sense of agency to craft a new African 'self' in America. Tensions and contradictions among local and global realities create vivid insight into global forces that reshape women's lives. Although Eve is educated as a nurse, massive unemployment in her hometown drives her to seek greener pastures in America as a nanny to a Nigerian family. Through flashbacks, she narrates the environmental devastation of her community such as, poverty, illness, and social pathologies that disproportionately affect women. She follows updates in the media about the crisis back home:

> Forty years it took for our story to reach the front pages of the *Times: Nigerian Delta Women in Oil Company Standoff*. The women had occupied Summit Oil's terminal, the report said. If their demands were not met, they would strip naked, and this was a shaming gesture, according to a local custom.
>
> (2010b 170)

These developments are authentic because, in 2002, Nigerian women activists in the Niger Delta staged a peaceful and successful protest that was reported in the international media. Eve's consciousness unfolds from the translocal perspective through reflection on life in America and news from Nigeria that sparks her growing solidarity with the women back home. Similar to the female protagonist in "A Temporary Position", Eve constantly makes comparisons between Nigeria and America: "under the black-blue New Jersey sky, I thought that living in America was exactly what it was like to live in a mortuary" (173).

Despite her unhappiness she plans to legalize her undocumented status by acquiring a green card through sponsorship. Even though she is a trained nurse, she realizes she has no future in Nigeria: "Most nurses I graduated with were selling bottled water, bathing soap, tinned milk for a living" (2010b: 171). Her 'gaze' is always shifting from recollections of the troubling past, while battling culture shock and racial difference in America. Eve wonders:

> Will living here be different for me? Sometimes a shop assistant follows me in a store, and I want to turn and scream, "If not for the havoc your people have wreaked in my country, would I be here taking shit from you?! Then, on a day like this, I think of the guerilla politicos in my country, petroleum hawkers, who treat the land and the people of the Niger Delta like waste matter. I look around the park, see the trees I can't name, clear skies, smell the clean air in New Jersey that is supposedly polluted, and think, "Well Gawd bless America."
>
> (2010b: 182)

Eve juxtaposes the dangerous pollution in the Niger Delta through vivid images of environmental damage that motivated the women's protest movement:

> In my hometown we had rainbow-colored water. It tasted of the oil that had leaked into our well. Bathing water we fetched from a creek. This smelled of dead crayfish. Our rivers were also dead. When rain fell, it rusted rooftops, shriveled plants. People who drank rainwater swore that it burnt permanent holes in their stomachs.
>
> (2010b: 175–176)

There are many layers of environmental destruction with massive consequences for the livelihoods of people in Eve's community, "The land was now sinking ... from the center of town we could smell burning mixed with petrol" (176). These recollections are critical issues for Nigeria in the global age, with unfavorable implications for young people like Eve.

The couple that Eve works for are both doctors, and Dr (Mrs) Darego, ironically, is seeking to regularize her legal status in order to work professionally. In this way, Atta draws attention to the difficulties that Nigerian/African women may face abroad even though they are educated. At first appearance, the Daregos have achieved the American Dream, but Eve gradually realizes the paradoxical realities and contradictions in their lives. Their marriage is empty and marred by gender conflict and emotional distance. Atta vividly illustrates the way that Eve comes to terms with the 'Western gaze' towards Africa, sadly through the behaviors of the Darego children, for whom she is a nanny.

Eve notes the Americanized behavior of the Darego children, who confidently tout media stereotypes and distorted images of Africa. When Eve meets them:

> their expressions were Who-are-you? and What-d' you want? Their accents were wanna, gonna, shoulda ... Daniel tells Eve: I sawed the picture of Africa ... And the boy had no hair, and his belly was all swelled up, and he lived in a hut with, um no, windows and I don't like Africa. Africa women have droopy boobies.
>
> (2010b: 174)

"News from Home" skillfully portrays common Western perceptions of Africa, created through a media-driven lens of ignorance, racism, cultural bias, and mis-education. The children exhibit many questionable behaviors, such as using their parents' first names, rudeness, and inappropriate comments. Such behaviors may be common in Western spaces, but in the Nigerian cultural environment it is unacceptable. Eve is puzzled and tries to correct the children's descriptions of Nigeria/Africa. Their behaviors reveal weak and ineffective parenting in the hybridized and confusing African diaspora, especially since the children are second-generation Nigerians with American citizenship. The story comes to a dramatic end when Dr (Mrs) Darego shows Eve a photograph of the demonstrators from her hometown, which she printed from the Internet. The women in the photograph are Eve's mother, their leader Madam Queen, and others whom she knows. The 'news from home' is jubilant on all fronts because "They've brought Summit Oil's operations to a standstill! The company is negotiating with them." (2010b: 198). These unprecedented events parallel the emergence of Eve's new identity in America. From this point, women's awakened consciousness, both at home and abroad, are merged in feminist expression through solidarity, agency, and strength.

The kaleidoscopic prism of fluid and shifting realities and perceptions in the African diaspora give rise to inner reflection and examination of oneself. "News from Home" suggests potential for positive outcomes in the lives of women when they inspire each other to transform society as well as themselves.

"On Monday of Last Week" is a selection from Chimamanda Ngozi Adichie's short fiction collection *The Thing Around Your Neck*. Like other fictional works by Adichie a Nigerian female immigrant takes center stage as a woman searching for happiness in America. Misra and Shrivastava support this when they assert: "Adichie takes a particular care in telling some personal and painful stories of dislocated Nigerian women who have relocated to America through marriage, and may be seeking better education and jobs–or have some obscure dreams to fill" (2009: 188). Like the women in "A Temporary Position" and "News from Home", she is educated, with a master's degree, pursuing a better life in the African diaspora. Like many women, she seeks validation from others, driven by loneliness and failed American dreams with her Nigerian husband. The title speaks to the temporal marker of the protagonists' awakening to the possibility of a new identity.

The Nigerian cultural environment is Kamara's frame of reference to navigate an uncertain identity in America. She begins her journey in the African diaspora as a baby sitter to escape a lifeless marriage. Her observations belie culture shock through her interactions with the privileged couple she works for who are bi-racial. Through a steady flow of puzzling experiences, she pieces together appropriate behaviors, protocols and awkward realities. The new experiences are an initiation into *otherness*. She quickly learns not to use the term "half-caste" to refer to bi-racial people. She has never heard this term before and is dumbfounded. As a new immigrant, Kamara is unaware of pejorative categories of 'naming', which she is guilty of in using the term "half-caste".

When she is interviewed for the job by the husband, who is Caucasian, he is surprised that she speaks such good English. Of course this annoys her because it unpacks common misperceptions and ignorance about the 'African other', ignorance and she thinks to herself: "his assumption that English was somehow his personal property" (Adichie 2009: 76). Experiences such as these illustrates that, however subtle, African immigrants, as transnational subjects begin to see themselves through the eyes of others. Some of the culture clashes occurs in relation to the young boy she cares for. When she is informed of her duties, she is cautioned to never spank Josh because the parents did not believe in abuse as discipline. Kamara finds these views incomprehensible and wanted to say, "abuse is a different thing..." (78) She'd heard news reports about Americans doing things like putting out cigarettes on their children's skin. She regrets taking the job.

The most puzzling experience in her new job is the absence of the child's mother who is African-American. She is never seen because she is an artist who spends most of her time in the basement. Atta dramatizes the entrance of Tracy, and the attraction felt by Kamara as a turning point in her confusing and lonely life. The title "On Monday of Last Week" is a backward glance into the life of the protagonist and the expectation of a relationship outside her marriage.

The 'gaze' turns to Kamara's life in Nigeria and the disillusionment of her shattered American dreams. These recollections suggest that she made poor choices in the search for marital security and a new life abroad. She remembers how she met her husband at university, married him and admits that "what drew her was the way he looked at her with awed eyes, eyes that made her like herself" (Adichie 2009: 83). When Tobechi leaves Nigeria for America, he is expected to work for two years, acquire a green card and send for her. Unfortunately, six years pass before he sends for her and like the Nigerian female immigrants in "A Temporary Position" and "News from Home" she is put off by the "staleness of the air" (84) that foreshadow her empty marriage. When contrasting their relationship in Nigeria she observes that, "Now, their silences were awkward, but she told herself that things would get better, they had been apart a long time, after all. In bed, she felt nothing except for the rubbery friction of skin against skin... (85).

She asks herself whether Tobechi is the same person she knew in Nigeria, and is annoyed at what she finds most troubling because he, "had begun to talk in that false accent that made her want to slap his face" (Adichie 2009: 85). She doesn't understand his unfamiliar behaviors and he appears to her as a sad empty version of his former self. These unsettling feelings and disappointment leads to eventual boredom and the desperate search for a job, just to escape the situation. Misra and Shrivasta confirm the nature of Kamara's problems with her new life in America:

> The initial culture shock after 'dislocation' opens up the process of disillusionment, which gradually affects both their energy and psyche and they start suffering from loneliness, despair, disappointment, psychological trauma and identity crisis. Sometimes this even makes them regret leaving their homeland.
>
> (Adichie 2009: 188)

Although this observation is made with reference to Adichie's story "The Thing Around Your Neck", Kamara in "On Monday of Last Week" exhibits similar responses to dislocation and unhappiness in America.

Atta has skillfully woven a story of alienation, eroded identity, and personal loss, narrated from the vantage point of the female 'gaze' from the diaspora. The search for a new life in America has unraveled empty longings and flawed self-perception in the protagonist. The author draws a parallel between the way that Kamara responds to the 'gaze' of others: first from her husband back in Nigeria and later, from her female employer, Tracy. This is very sad because her gender identity is essentially a reflection of others' perceptions rather than healthy feelings of self-esteem and acceptance. Themes of self-worth connect to the story's title, "On Monday of Last Week" because after meeting Tracy for the first time, she comes alive to the compliments and the invitation to pose naked as an artists' model. She is attracted to Tracy and recalls that: "Her voice was deep and her womanly body was fluid" (Adichie 2009: 87). She imagines Tracy whispering her name repeatedly in her ear, "while their bodies swayed to the music of the name" (89).

"On Monday of Last Week" captures the emotional dilemma of Kamara whose expectations for a relationship abruptly plummets when another female captures the attention of Tracy as a potential artists model. The uncertainties of life in the African diaspora may spill over into romantic interludes for lonely and unhappy immigrant women. The story evokes recollection of the ambiguous emotions between Sissie and Marija, a lonely German woman in Ama Ata Aidoo's *Our Sister Killjoy* (1977). In this work, Marija makes unmistakable sexual advances by attempting to kiss Sissie. Interestingly, the suggestion of a lesbian relationship does not materialize in either work but both authors introduce a kind of shadowy world where lonely women stir romantic expressions with their own gender. "On Monday of Last Week" is an understated account of the inner journey of a Nigerian woman that ends on a sad note of empty emotion.

In conclusion, Adichie's and Atta's short fiction convey intertextual elements of diaspora journeys in London and America. The fluid and transformative experiences of migration reshape women's identities within multinational spaces. Although the African diaspora in foreign settings may offer opportunities for employment and success, abrasive encounters of racial otherness are difficult to navigate. Perceptions of life in Nigeria, viewed through a diasporic lens, creates more confusion for the women although for Eve, in "News from Home", the situation in her hometown is a source of strength and feminist agency to change her life. For the protagonist in "A Temporary Position" her life suggests liminality as she weathers her status as *other*, perceived as a better choice than returning to Nigeria. Adichie's "On Monday of Last Week" illustrates how the depths of loneliness may push women into uncertain waters of confusion and self- effacement.

Another connecting thread of the works is that all of the Nigerian women are educated although the stories confirm that issues of race, class and gender mediate women's choices and opportunities for success. The women have accepted employment that is beneath their qualifications, causing boredom and more conflicting emotions. Adichie and Atta highlight the unfortunate realities of post-colonial conditions that adversely influence the lives of African women in the global age. There is never an easy answer to complex issues that occur in cross- cultural settings where African women are marginalized as *other*. Finally, African women that relocate into transcultural settings must (re)negotiate their relationship to Africa, hopefully in ways that develop a strong sense of agency and female empowerment.

Works cited

Adichie, Chimamanda Ngozi. "On Monday of Last Week". *The Thing Around Your Neck*. Canada. Alfred A. Knopf. 2009.
Aidoo, Ama Ata. *No Sweetness Here*. New York. The Feminist Press. 1970.
────── *Our Sister Killjoy: Or Reflections of a Black-Eyed Squint*. Lagos/ New York. Nok Press. 1977.
────── *The Girl Who Can and Other Stories*, London. Heinemann. African Writers Series, 1997.
────── *Diplomatic Pounds*. London. Ayebia Clarke Publishing. 2012.
Atta, Sefi. *Everything Good Will Come*. Northampton. Interlink Books. 2005.
────── "A Temporary Position". *News from Home*. Northampton. Interlink Books. 2010a.

———— "News from Home". *News from Home*. Northampton. Interlink Books. 2010b.

————. *Swallow*. Northampton. Interlink Books. 2010c.

Boyce-Davies, Carol. *Black Women Writing and Identity: Migrations of the Subject*. London and New York. Routeledge. 1994.

Emenyonu, Ernest. *African Literature Today* 31. London. James Currey. 2013. pp. 1–8.

Ezeigbo, Akachi Adimora. *Rhythm of Life: Stories of Modern Nigeria*. London. Karnak House. 1992.

———— *Echoes in the Mind*. Lagos. Foundation.1994.

———— *Rituals and Departures*. London. Karnak House. 1996.

———— *Fractures and Fragments*. Ikeja. Lantern Books. 2006.

———— *Magic Breast Bags*. Ibadan. University Press. 2019.

Feldner, Maximillian. *Narrating the New African Diaspora: twenty-first Century Literature in Context*. New York. Palgrave Macmillan. 2019.

Habila, Helon. "The Future of African Literature". ALA Presidential Address (2018). *Journal of the African Literature Association* Volume. 13, Issue 1, 2019. pp.153–162.

Jyothirmai, D. and Sree Ramesh. "Lawless/news from Home: Womanist Perspectives in Select Short Stories of Sefi Atta". *Journal of the African Literature Association*. Volume 9, Summer/Fall 2015. pp. 52–74.

Maitrayee, Misra and Manish Shrivastava. "Dislocation, Memory & Identity in *The Thing Around Your Neck*. A Companion to Chimamanda Ngozi Adichie. ed. Ernest Emenyonu. London. James Currey and Boydell and Brewer. 2017. pp. 185–197.

Evaristo, Bernadine. *Girl, Woman, Other*. New York. Grove Press. 2019.

Sackeyfio, Rose. "Diaspora Identities in Short Fiction by Chimamanda Ngozi Adichie and Sefi Atta". *African Literature Today 3: Writing Africa in the Short Story*. ed. Ernest Emenyonu. London. James Currey. 2013. 102–104.

————."Recasting Sisterhood and its Ambiguities". *Writing Contemporary Nigeria: How Sefi Atta Illuminates African Culture and Tradition*. ed. Walter Collins, III. New York. Cambria Press. 2015. pp. 41–58.

Unigwe., Chika. *On Black Sisters' Street*. London. Jonathan Cape. 2009.

———— *Better Never Than Late*. Lagos. Cassava Republic. 2019.

8 There's no place like home
Memory and identity in *A Bit of Difference* by Sefi Atta

Contemporary African migration into Western spaces has increased steadily over the course of the late twentieth century to a more dramatic exodus from the continent in the global arena of the twenty-first century. In the search for economic advancement, education, and greater opportunities for success, African women émigrés in Europe and America must navigate and renegotiate their identities to reconcile their perceptions and reconnections to *home* and family. This chapter interrogates the complexities of these relationships and conflicts in Sefi Atta's latest novel *A Bit of Difference* (2013), through analysis of the female protagonist's life in Europe. It will trace the protagonist's return to Africa and will illuminate the impact of cultural hybridity on the search for a place called *home*.

In conventional terms, coming-of-age tales capture youthful transitions to adulthood, and chronicle new realities, changing identities, and alternating status in the world. The idea of unconditional acceptance and return to one's home from abroad frames a major dilemma for the lead character in the novel. Although diaspora settings represent a space for advancement, economic stability, and material rewards, transnational/hybrid identities of African women illustrate the ruptured and contested features of these locales as they reconfigure relationships to African cultural norms and expectations.

African women writers have explored the impact of migration on the lives of females in transnational spaces in early works of Buchi Emecheta such as *In the Ditch* (1994) and Ama Ata Aidoo's *Our Sister Killjoy* (1977), *Changes* in (1991 and *Diplomatic Pounds* (2012). In the exploration of splintered existence of women living abroad, *On Black Sisters' Street* (2009) by Chika Unigwe, and Akachi Adimora Ezeigbo's *Trafficked* (2008) examine the lives of African women who take on new identities as sex workers in Europe. In addition, Chimamanda Ngozi Adichie's short story collection *The Thing Around Your Neck* (2010) and

DOI: 10.4324/9781003219323-9

her novel *Americanah* (2013) represent fictional works that foreground realistic, insightful, and vivid portrays of cultural hybridity within transnational spaces. Sefi Atta effectively captures diverse experiences and challenges of diaspora life for African women in her short story collection *News from Home* (2010). Moreover, this genre of literature chronicles the expansion of conventional themes and motifs that have characterized African women's writing since the first generation of women writers commanded new spaces in the African literary world from the 1960's until the present.

In *A Bit of Difference*, Sefi Atta chronicles the immigrant experiences of a Nigerian woman seeking *home* as a place of return. Having been educated in London, her life is at a crossroads because her diaspora life has usurped her cultural identity and Nigerian traditional role as wife and mother, roles that would firmly gain her acceptance and reconnection to home. The centrality of motherhood as a normative aspect in African familial structures is skillfully recast as a familiar theme that forms the nexus of the protagonist's conflict. Through her inability to meet the expectations of a culturally defined role as an African woman, perceptions and connections to *home* becomes a contested space whose boundaries the protagonist must traverse.

In addition to juxtaposing notions of home with realities of failed expectations of her family, *A Bit of Difference* simulates a coming-of-age odyssey into African womanhood through the binaries of tradition and modernity and a larger diaspora lens of hyphenated identities. African traditions, though never static and unchanging, represent the cultural *homespace* the protagonist must balance with her diaspora existence. Her life abroad is a tangle of contradictions and confusion that is a common feature of the immigrant experience. As a product of both worlds, Adeola, the female character, must come to terms with what it means to be a Nigerian woman both at *home* and abroad.

Sefi Atta's *A Bit of Difference* unfolds the journey of Adeola Adeniran, a 39-year-old Nigerian woman, unmarried and at odds with her life in London, and most of all in conflict with herself. Finding a solution to this dilemma is imperative, because in her culture women are expected to marry early. Her future in London is unfulfilling and uncertain because of the unfavorable racial environment and the contradictions of immigrant identity. The novel is a coming-of-age apologue of how Adeola attests her Nigerian cultural identity that gradually surface in the spatio-temporal locus of Europe and Nigeria. The contested reality she faces in the transnational space(s) of London is mirrored in the tensions she endures as an unmarried woman who circumvents marriage and motherhood. These tensions are expressed succinctly by Marlene De La Cruz-Guzman, who notes that Adeola,

> is unhappy in her professional life abroad, but she is also reluctant to return to Lagos to face expectations of marriage and motherhood that she has so far evaded. She has peace in her Western refuge, but she lacks community and is lonely as a consequence.
>
> (2015: 6)

Adeola's character, and the assertion of her Nigerian identity, crystallize in the alienating environment of London, where she grew up during her teens. Although she does not fully belong in either London or Nigeria, early in the novel she says to a British co-worker that: "She has never had any doubts about her identity, although other people have. She has yet to encounter an adequate description of her status overseas. Resident alien is the closest. She definitely does not see herself as British. Perhaps she is a Nigerian expatriate in London" (Atta 2013: 5). The message conveyed in this exchange indicates that her presence in London invariably creates an uncomfortable racial and ethnic dynamic of self-definition in a hostile environment. The difficult surroundings of many African immigrants not only raise questions of identity, but also force them into a seemingly endless navigation of complex relationships in foreign spaces, within their communities and with people back home. The spatio-temporal dimensions of the story highlight the tension between the local and global elements, the individual and society, and amplify the decentering of the unified self. Sefi Atta interrogates the metamorphic landscape of Western spaces that nurture individualism in the behaviors of African immigrants. This represents the underlying truth of the novel in that hybrid identities among Africans living in the West are unavoidable, and although the lonely journeys into foreign space is a universal phenomenon of human experience, in the case of African people it acquires the added dimension of race as they are permanently cast as the other within European borders.

One of the reasons Deola is gradually drawn toward Nigeria is her growing contemplation and scrutiny of the 'plastic' Nigerians in her circle of friends in London. Throughout the novel her views and perceptions of Nigerian identity are refocused and sharpened to a sense of national allegiance and connection to home. She observes that, among Nigerians in London, their British accents are indistinguishable from Europeans and she notes that one of her friends, called Bandele, "sounded completely English and all she knew about Nigerians who spoke that way is that they looked down on Nigerian's who didn't" (Atta 2013: 32). Many contemporary African writers note these unfavorable behaviors within immigrant fictional works, as it represents a cogent theme that recurs in new writing in the global age. Moreover, in the effort to fit in, many African immigrants adopt awkward coping mechanisms, and leading among these is the use of acquired American or British accents. Nigerian characters in Atta's *News from Home,* Adichie's *Americanah,* and stories from *The Thing Around Your Neck,* as well as Bulawayo's *We Need New Names* (2013), illustrate this characteristic.

Deola recalls that: "some expats couldn't tell one Nigerian from another" (Atta 2013: 32). In another very telling conversation with her best friend, Bandele, Deola tells him she is going home to Nigeria and he asks her, "Where is home?" She responds "Where else?" He quickly retorts that "Nigeria is not *my* home and that he has not been back in so long until he'd probably catch dengue fever the moment he returned to *that country*" (37). He refers to Nigerians as savages. Bandele is a frustrated writer, social misfit, and a victim of depression. Deola tells herself not to worry about him because "Every Nigerian she knows abroad is to some degree broken" (38). Other Nigerians she knows describe her friend as "the bobo who went mad because he couldn't accept the fact that he was black" (39). For Deola, "His ridicule of Nigerians is hard to take, and she once attributed it to the sort of self loathing that only English public school schools can impart on a young impressionable foreign mind" (40).

This observation highlights the plight of many immigrant children who are products of socialization and schooling in foreign spaces. These experiences evoke recollections of Tsitsi Dangaremgba's classic work *Nervous Conditions* (1988), which skillfully reveals the negative impact of foreign education on young African children. The novel illustrates that, for many African children, Western education may easily become a form mis-education resulting in self-loathing. Other works that depict identity crisis is Adichie in *Americanah,* where Ifemelu's nephew Dike attempts to commit suicide as a result of extreme alienation, racial profiling, and poor coping mechanisms.

Atta's depiction of Nigerian immigrants in London who grapple with ambiguous identities and negative perceptions of *home* resonates in the work of Stuart Hall in the seminal publication *Modernity: An Introduction to Modern Societies* (1996), and with regard to the formation of new identities in contemporary societies, he attributes identity conflict among immigrant populations to a "complex of processes and forces of change, which for convenience can be summed up under the term "globalization... National identities are declining but *new* identities of hybridity are taking their place" (1996: 619). As a feature of globalization, massive movement of people across geographical borderlands has created overlapping boundaries of identity that clearly may affect both genders. *A Bit of Difference* illuminates the idea that, regardless of the extent to which an African immigrant woman identifies with her country, "diaspora women are caught between...ambiguous pasts, and futures. They connect and disconnect, forget and remember, in complex strategic ways... The lived experiences of diaspora women thus involve painful difficulty in mediating discrepant worlds" (Clifford 1994: 314). In recent decades the dramatic increase of African migrant populations is being transformed by flows and linkages among diverse groups within an expanded landscape of fluctuating identities.

Atta's commitment to social realism effectively captures these kinds of changes through the portrayal of behaviors and difficult choices of the female protagonist. Sefi Atta elucidates the vagaries of racial discrimination and the antagonistic encounters that splinters the lives of Nigerian and other African immigrants. In London Deola becomes painfully aware of her race as a defining marker of her identity by Europeans. Like all African people living in Africa, her identity derives from her ethnicity, not her skin color. In *African and American: West Africans in Post-Civil Rights America* (2014), Marilyn Halter and Violet Johnson include a succinct and vivid account of a Nigerian immigrant coming to terms with a racialized identity in America:

> As soon as I arrived in USA, (1990), I underwent a singular transformation, the consequences of which have circumscribed my life ever since: I BECAME BLACK!. The difference is that as soon as I entered the United States my otherwise complex, multidimensional, and rich human identity became completely reduced to a simple, one dimensional, impoverished nonhuman identity. I am saying, in other words, that to become "black in the United States is to enter a sphere where there is no differentiation, no distinction, and no variation.
>
> (2014: 9)

Although the testimonial above contextualizes the African immigrant collisions in America, it speaks to racialized identity that is superimposed onto African ethnic identity in Europe as well. Yogita Goyal asserts the timeliness of new discourse about race in a global context and, with reference to authors like Sefi Atta, Chimamanda Ngozi Adichie, and others, notes that such discussions: "inaugurates an important and long overdue conversation about the specificity of a Nigerian experience of racialization in the US and the UK, tying it firmly to both class and gender" (2004: xi). The negative portrayal of black people outside Africa can be daunting, and may force African people to redefine themselves as a coping mechanism and survival strategy within new spaces of the West.

For Deola and other African immigrants, the first distinguishing mark of otherness is skin color, followed by their accent. Atta describes in colorful terms the mangled and awkward attempts of many immigrants to fit in by developing affectations and exaggerated speech. The experience of disjointed and confusing racialized identity mandates newly acquired thought patterns and behaviors. Deola recalls that when she began schooling in London she tried to blend in by "rounding her vowels" and speaking "phonetics". Early in the novel when she visits America, the woman she works for thinks Deola is British because of her acquired accent.

Years later, with a new consciousness and acceptance of her Nigerian identity, she contemplates such pretentious behaviors in her past and in the lives of her fellow Nigerians in London. Deola recalls that she used to be just like them in that:

> despite their academic competence, they were so averse to seeing themselves as subjugated or victimized in any way that to say race had any relevance to them was an admission too lowly to contemplate. In fact, if anyone was in the habit of bringing up racial issues Deola (in the past) might have accused them of having an inferiority complex. She notes that at home in Nigeria she is "virtually color free and she hopes to remain that way.
>
> (Atta 2013: 57)

When she visits Nigeria, her brother tells her: "That's one good thing about this place. We don't have any of that racialism rubbish....she replies that she sees too much of it abroad" (58). These ideas represent a fresh perspective on Deola's unsatisfying life in London, and the realization of her battered identity as a displaced Nigerian.

Adichie expresses discomforting perceptions of racial dynamics that are laced throughout her latest novel *Americanah* and in a *Vogue* interview on March 17, 2015 called "I Wanted to Claim My Own Name" she recalls that "I only became black when I came to America" and she reiterates that in America, her experience "is always shaped by race" and the same is true for Africans living in Europe. As a mirror of real-world issues and contemporary conflicts, the younger breed of African writers who are based in the West are exploring race as a timely motif that capture twenty-first century discomfort within modern landscapes of dichotomized existence.

As the novel progresses, Deola's consciousness of how her race matters in London becomes all too apparent. She works for an NGO that supports development projects in Africa. While visiting Nigeria she must interview two local organizations and give a report that will determine whether or not they will be funded. Through interacting with her British employers, she begins to see Nigeria and Africa through the negative, stereotypical, and racialized lens of Europeans. Her transnational gaze sparks the awareness of her ethnic identity in the UK, political consciousness, and reconnection to home that forms a clear vision of herself as an African woman. These experiences open her eyes to the contradictions within her diaspora life and cause her to question her employment with the NGO.

Further, Deola describes the hostile environment of her workplace as "Stuckupsdale" and the hierarchy of discrimination towards immigrant employees that she observes. Some of her fellow employees were tolerated while others were dismissed within a climate of overall lack of respect for diverse backgrounds of people. She describes the inappropriate treatment of an elderly Nigerian employee by her British employers who speak to him in condescending tones and casually address him as "Jimmy", something unthinkable in the Nigerian context because of deeply ingrained respect for elders as a cultural practice. She recalls polite greetings to the man whom she addresses as Mr Ojo and says that: "without him, there were days she could have wept walking through that door" (Atta 2013: 155). Deola reveals that "back then, bigotry was often cryptic, like a missed punch line in a joke. It always took her a moment to catch on" (154). Atta articulates forms of covert racism and alienating experiences of othering that codify diaspora subjectivity in the life of the protagonist.

Deola encounters more abrasive treatment and knows immediately that " it couldn't possibly be her wool coats that gave her a constant feeling of being weighed down... Apart from the 'braids were unprofessional business'" (2013: 154), she had a somewhat unpleasant encounter at a pension fund when a manager looked at her palms and said "you're two-toned", and another at a bank, when she arrived at the reception with audit files and said, "I'm here for the audit," and the receptionist replied, "Deliveries are through the side entrance"(2013: 152). The emotional brutality of racism its takes toll on Deola so that perceptions of 'home' take on new meaning in the security of Lagos and her fellow Nigerians. Even though her brother and others complain and point out problems in Nigeria, she is drawn to the local flavor of uniquely Nigerian behaviors, peculiarities, and nuanced encounters at home. For example, Deola describes a colorful character in the airport whose comical and animated conversations captivate her attention. She thinks to herself that "she cherishes her homecomings because of characters like him....She loves her fellow Nigerians ...and can't stop looking at him" (51). When her relatives ask routine questions about her flight, she admits to herself that she is "enjoying the proximity of their voices" (56). In addition, Atta pointedly contrasts unbalanced, distorted, and stereotypical news items about Nigeria when Deola reads the Sunday newspapers: "The headlines are about trade and politics, not the news she is used to reading about Nigeria overseas, which is about Internet fraud, drug traffickers, Islamic fundamentalism and armed militants in the Niger Delta" (56). Her senses are heightened to the pervasive nature of negative media representations of Nigeria, and Africa in general, and she gains this perspective during her visit home.

Later, while Deola is still in Lagos, she reflects upon the lives of her local counterparts as follows:

> Of the Ikoyi crowd, she is one of the few living abroad. The rest fly in and out and educate their children overseas...They say things are bad in Nigeria, but there is money in the oil industry despite the grand larceny that goes on. There is money in the telecommunications and banking industries. There is money in the churches and non-governmental organizations. There is money for those who own their own professional practices. And for those who do not care to go through the normal apprenticeships or be burdened with public accountability, there are political positions in the Third Republic.
>
> (2013: 63)

Essentially, her observations confirm that, despite glaring contradictions, corruption, and economic inequality at home, it is possible to carve out a life where many Nigerians can experience the best of both worlds.

In addition, when Deola contemplates the term "brain drain" she thinks of it as suspicious:

> She has always thought there are enough brains in Africa, at least in Lagos. People who may not do much for the common good, but they achieve so much for themselves. She runs into old friends, most of whom are married with children, and marvels at their accomplishments-lawyers who are jewelry designers on the side,

doctors who just happen to be manufacturing beauty creams, accountants who produce Nollywood films. They make opportunities overseas look like a joke.

(2013: 87).

These reflections on the success, creativity, and resourcefulness of her contemporaries based in Nigeria signal a balanced perspective on the reality of making a living in Africa. These perceptions display an important contrast to complaints by Nigerians visiting from abroad. It is common to hear the doom and gloom descriptions, caustic, and one-dimensional assessments about what is *not working* in Nigeria and other developing African economies. Her brother succinctly conveys these viewpoints and, in a conversation with Deola, he describes contrasting realities of home and London: "Abroad you can have it all – money, good health and security – and it's as if someone is chipping away at your backbone every day with that racialism rubbish. I can't deal with that" (2013: 195).

These ideas weigh very heavily on Deola's loneliness for home and family as she casts her mind back to how it all began and makes a decision to quit her job. The rush of new thoughts represents her newly awakened sense of displacement, contradictions in her life, and the misguided agenda of the NGO that offers *aid* to local organizations back home. Deola recalls interviewing for the job (with the NGO) and how uncomfortable she felt speaking English. She had asked herself: "What was the point of speaking English? What was the point of working for an organization that hired Africans like herself, who, in the process of being refined, could no longer think for themselves?" (2013: 175). She tells her Nigerian friend that "she will talk to them, and if they can't be open to an idea that involves a community of Africans being independent, then maybe she is working for the wrong organization" (152).

At this point she decides to move back to Nigeria but is forced to remain superficial and full of pretense till the end. When giving notice to leave her job:

> She tells them how much her trip to Nigeria woke her up to the fact that she misses home and she ought to go back for good instead of contributing to the brain drain. Even to her own ears she sounds fake and she is tired of rounding her vowels. Rounding her vowels hurts her mouth. She wonders what would happen if Nigerians refused to speak phonetics for one day. Would their worlds fall apart? Would they realize that it would be just as absurd for them as

Nigerians, to speak in Chinese accents to keep up with the direction in which the world was going?

(2013: 175–176)

The incongruent realities of dislocation in London come sharply into focus when Deola returns home to Lagos for a memorial to her father. The women in her family gently chide her in her family to return and assume a traditional role of wife and mother. In Nigeria, socially prescribed roles for women define their identity in society and womanhood is synonymous with motherhood. Among her people her identity as a woman takes precedence over her racial identity abroad, which ruptures her cultural moorings. The women in her family are wondering when she will return, get married, and settle down. Her mother's friends are described as "still trying to persuade her to come home" (2013: 118). One of her aunts wants to know whether she is ready to settle down.

When thinking back to her solitary existence in London, Deola remembers that "she held onto her independence there even as her independence began to look more like loneliness" (2013: 88). Among her extended family her maternal aunts advise her to "forget about her career and focus on having a child" (126). Another aunt is even more persistent and tells Deola in no uncertain terms: "Make you just hurry up and born *pikin*. All this book *wey* you *dey* learn London… at least born *pikin* if you no want marry….It's you we are waiting for now. Let us see our successors before we die… All this career, career will get you nowhere as a woman" (126). Sefi Atta skillfully renders the protagonists' journey home to a space of belonging and fulfillment. Tanure Ojaide, in "Migration, Globalization and Recent African Literature" notes that in contemporary African literature about African migrants "as the characters that leave Africa for one reason or the other express relief, so do those characters that go back to Africa have initial problems and eventual self-fulfillment. Generally there is a new type of alienation" (2008: 46). Deola overcomes discordant energies about her life, but the impulse towards motherhood unfolds very slowly through encouragement from female relatives and unexpected romantic involvement.

Atta weaves an ironic twist in the novel because Deola meets a man she is attracted to and accidently becomes pregnant. The dramatic turn of events is timely in the structure of the novel and cements her resolve to return home for good. She returns to London for the last time as a woman transformed by the prospect of motherhood. By the end of the novel, her Nigerian cultural identity is recast through the new life she is nurturing and her growing baby is a symbol of renewed and reinvigorated existence. Her pregnancy suggests the merging of her past, present, and future. Deola has come full circle as she anticipates her new life as a parent: "She thinks of her growing child as a friend, a friend she is getting acquainted with. She must have grown up to some extent because she is able to put her fears aside, and what might have been a sense of failure is now a determination to be worthy of being a mother" (Atta 2013: 213).

Deola has come to terms with what it means to be a Nigerian woman at home and abroad and is finally at peace with her life. The pressure from her family sinks deeply in her mind after her visit to Nigeria. As she continues to put her life in perspective, the negative portrayal of Africa in London is increasingly distasteful and totally unacceptable. In her last days in London:

> she watches a Hollywood film that takes place in an imaginary African country. The usual elements are in the film: the benevolent missionary priest; the hopeful expatriate and cynical foreign journalist who has a change of conscience; the sidekick African intellectual and the corrupt local politician. Red-eyed African military men drive around in trucks brandishing machine guns. Arrogant UN troops are unsympathetic to the hungry refugees and barefoot children. There is much drumming and singing and panoramic shots of green hills. It is painful to watch, almost as if a mass sacrifice has taken place so the journalist and the expatriate can fall in love.
>
> (2013: 213)

Deola recalls that "she has never recognized this Africa and is increasingly dissatisfied with what she sees on television in the news. She recalls that normally she would allow herself to be seduced, but not today" (213). The shifting perceptions of the protagonist and her strong reactions signals intolerance of racialized existence in London and rejection of the "single story" of Africa projected from a Western gaze of incoherent and distorted images.

The novel ends on a note of promise for a new life in Nigeria, symbolized by motherhood, because her baby represents the future. Deola will be married and achieve a sense of wholeness and stability unthinkable in the transnational and fracturing environment of London because 'there's no place like home'. Adeola's coming-of-age experience is propelled by rejection of diaspora confusion, the disquieting contradictions of her charity work with the NGO, and the beginning of a new life as a mother. As a diaspora subject, Deola's balancing act between two worlds of difference is a caveat in the modern arena of globalization. The ongoing erosion of cultural identity is an unsettling consequence of the massive globalized movement of people, which creates new layers of contested realities in post-modern spaces. There are no easy or comfortable solutions to the complexity of social, economic, and political forces that act upon people as social beings. Extended family networks, responsibilities, and kinship ties that are intrinsic to African 'traditional' culture are very binding, but these are changing in the global arena of migration and displacement.

Atta's commitment to social realism effectively captures these kinds of changes through the behaviors and difficult choices of the female protagonist. The novel is a vivid rendering of global dimensions, as the character's fragmented lives, identities, and harmonious existence lies at the mercy of local and global tensions and transformations. Nigerians and other African nationals living abroad who disconnect from their homeland is a powerful motif that binds Sefi Atta's works as a chronicle of diaspora pressures in the twenty-first century. Sefi Atta has crafted a compelling fictional account that portrays the complexity of educated and successful women redefining their identity as they negotiate ambiguous and antagonistic realities in their lives.

For the female protagonist in the novel, migration to Europe represents upward mobility, independence, and access to the trappings of Western life. Unfortunately, cultural dissonance, alienation, and racism enmesh her life within a disconnected space of uncertain outcomes. However, by the end of the novel Adeola Adeniran has come full circle as an African woman who cherishes her homeland and renews her commitment to live in Nigeria. An important message and strength of the novel lies in the exploration of the relationship between the African individual and society and the path toward liberation from the mystique and lure of the West. Thus, *A Bit of Difference* illuminates a woman's journey back home to a space of acceptance, belonging and fulfillment as a mother, while avoiding the constraints imposed by patriarchal expectations and norms for women.

Works cited

Adichie, Chimamanda. *The Thing Around Your Neck*. Toronto. Alfred A. Knopf. 2009.
—— *Americanah*. Toronto. Alfred A. Knopf. 2013.
—— "I Wanted to Claim my Own Name" *Vogue UK*. March 17, 2015.
Aidoo, Ama Ata. *Our Sister Killjoy: Or Reflections of a Black-Eyed Squint*. Lagos/New York. Nok Press. 1977.

——— *Changes a Love Story*. New York. The Feminist Press. 1991.
——— *Diplomatic Pounds & Other Stories*. UK. Ayebia Clarke Publishing, 2012.
Atta, Sefi. *Everything Good Will Come*. Northampton. Interlink Books. 2005.
——— _ *News from Home*. Northampton. Interlink Books. 2010.
——— *A Bit of Difference*. Northampton. Interlink Books. 2013.
Bulawayo, NoViolet. *We Need New Names*. Bulawayo, New York. Regan Arthur Books. 2013.
Clifford, James. "Further Inflections Toward Ethnographies of the Future". *Cultural Anthropology*. Vol. 9. No. 3. 1994. pp. 302–338.
Cruz-Guzman, Marlene De La. "Of Motherhood, Marriage, and Professionals". *Writing Contemporary Nigeria. How Sefi Atta Illuminates African Culture and Tradition*. Ed. Walter P. Collins, III. Amherst, MA. Cambria. 2015. pp. 3–40.
Dangaremgba, Tsitsi. *Nervous Conditions*. Seattle. Seal Press. 1988.
Emecheta, Buchi. *In the Ditch*. London. Heinemann.1994.
Ezeigbo, Akachi-Adimora. *Trafficked*. Lagos. Lantern Books. 2008.
Goyal, Yogita. "Africa and the Black Atlantic". *Research in African Literatures*. Vol. 45. No. 3. 2014. pp. v–xxv.
Hall, Stuart, et al. *Modernity: An Introduction to Modern Societies*. Oxford. Blackwell Publishers. 1996. pp. 596–632.
Halter, Marilyn and Violet Johnson. *African and American: West Africans in Post-Civil Rights America*. New York. New York University Press. 2014.
Ojaide, Tanure. "Migration, Globalization, and Recent African Literature". *World Literature Today*. March–April 2008. pp. 43–46.
Unigwe, Chika. *On Black Sisters' Street*. London. Jonathan Cape. 2009.

Conclusion

West African Women in the Diaspora: Narratives of Other Spaces, Other Selves, contextualizes the outpouring of contemporary African women's diaspora fiction. The works that are examined highlight the intertextual elements of diaspora themes that recur in women's fiction that spans the twentieth and twenty-first centuries in multi-local spaces of the West. This is the first publication exclusively devoted to West African women writers who live in the diaspora and produce compelling fictional works about life in translocal sites. The volume codifies the genre through interrogation of cogent transnational issues that plague the lives of African immigrant women. Literary analysis of the works in this book foreground diaspora themes as part of a new trajectory in the African novel as well as in short fictional works.

Post-colonial and feminist perspectives frame the analysis of the fiction and some of literature studied gestures to Afropolitan aesthetics. Compelling features of the novels and short fiction explored include the ways in which females navigate otherness, hybridity, notions of homeland, and women's contested cultural identity in spaces of the global north. *West African Women in the Diaspora: Narratives of Other Spaces, Other Selves,* presents a critical and carefully nuanced representation of interlocking forces that reposition, as well as transform, African women's identities across national and geographic boundaries. More broadly, Helon Habila applauds new directions in contemporary African literature that includes male and female writers:

> I see this new wave of diasporic African literature as providing a new possibility, a way forward for African literature in general. A way out of the endless loop of nationalism and anti-colonialism, which keeps us trapped within the very structures of power we seek to oppose or correct.

(2019: 159)

Conclusion 125

Collectively, the fictional works that are discussed forms a vivid and composite portrait of African women as they grapple with identity politics in the diasporic landscape.

Nigerian writers are represented prominently as a reflection of the robust production of fiction from writers that reside in the West. Their perspectives stem from having been educated abroad, which translates to deep insight that encapsulates a transnational 'gaze'. Maximillian Feldner in *Narrating the New Diaspora: 21st century Nigerian Literature in Context* (2019) says of contemporary Nigerian writers that they have

> left Nigeria to live abroad, and yet they remain attached to the country, often returning home permanently or for visits. Novels abroad engage with Nigeria but, due to the authors' international experiences and transcultural perspectives, their stories avoid parochialism and aggressive patriotism.
>
> (2019: 4)

In the same way, Ghanaian writers featured in the book are attracting critical acclaim and leading among them is Taiye Selasi, followed by Yaa Gyasi who published *Homegoing* in 2016 and *Transcendent Kingdom* in 2020.

The literature examined traces African women's literary history by linking the past to the present and spatio-temporality marks the inception of women's writing from the mid-nineteenth century till the global age. Emecheta's *Second Class Citizen* (1974) and Aidoo's *Our Sister Killjoy* (1977) (see Chapters 1 and 2) are post-colonial classics that share many concerns about African women migrants. Essentially, both works are defined as immigrant novels as well as conventional post-independence works because of polemical engagement that questions colonization and neo-colonialism in Nigeria and Ghana respectively.

Ato Quayson discusses divergent concerns of first-generation writers whose seminal novels express post-colonial disillusionment that appear in African literature from the late 1960s through the early 1980s (2019: 148). In contrast, third-generation women writers focus their works on,

> depictions of what it is to be a person of color navigating the dynamics of the existence within the West itself. In other words, the interest in the most widely-read new African writers is now no longer on what happens to the African located in Africa, but what happens to the African resident in London, New York, Edinbourgh, Berlin, or Rome who keeps dreaming nostalgically of Africa.
>
> (2019: 149)

These alternative realities have shifted the direction of the African novel as illustrated in the chapters that follow those on Buchi Emecheta and Ama Aidoo in the beginning of the book. Other salient features that unify the work are the exploration of racialized identities, and patriarchal structures, along with Afropolitan aesthetics. These issues are equally pervasive in the past and the present and suggest that many of the challenges that women encountered decades ago have never changed and, in some ways, have worsened for African immigrant women. To illustrate, the rise of anti-immigrant sentiment, draconian immigration laws, and decreased opportunities for non-Western migrants across Europe is a reality in the global age. Massive flows and movement of African populations into former colonial nations has exacerbated tensions between political entities of the global north and south.

Another change in the twenty-first-century landscape is the growth of large African ethnic communities in urban capitals in Europe and America, which may act as a safety net against alienation and isolation among migrant groups. The existence of ethnic associations, preservation of communal ties, celebration of holidays and other cultural events, is now a common feature of contemporary African diaspora life throughout the West, the Asian continent, and indeed throughout the world. Despite these positive cultural linkages, the diaspora-themed works in the book are realistic representations of racial otherness, social barriers, and the tensions that Africans experience in the West.

Moreover, a highly-successful novel like Adichie's masterful *Americanah* (2013) is essentially a treatise on racial dynamics in the USA that resonates the complexities of being 'black' in America as opposed to ethnic, national, and linguistic markers of African identity on the African continent. Adichie's ideas about blackness is a dramatic departure from minimal literary attention to relationships between the old and new African diaspora communities.

Chika Unigwe's *On Black Sisters' Street* (see Chapter 3) is a disturbing and gripping account of modern-day slavery between Nigeria and Belgium. The novel may be read as post-colonial discourse that foregrounds the ripe conditions for sex trafficking to flourish in Africa. International crime syndicates and their local African affiliates have perpetuated the commodification of black African bodies in the global market. The novel's allusion to the centuries' long Atlantic slave trade is a caveat that warns of African complicity in the trade, similar to the wholesale exportation of black female bodies in the past. Further, the insidious nature of patriarchal structures is equally entrenched in society today in the same way as in the past. The control of women's labor, sexuality, and autonomy is perpetuated through layers of socio-cultural norms and women's subordinate status is sometimes aided by women who internalize patriarchal attitudes. *On Black Sisters' Street* profiles two women characters who support the violation of women's bodies, especially the educated Madam in Belgium. A common feature in the lives of all the women is the centrality of Lagos as a site of vulnerability and danger.

Historically, all human societies practiced some form of servitude, and sex trafficking is a blight on Nigeria and other nations as it robs women of potential for a legitimate means of survival in the future. Further, the insidious nature of patriarchal structures is equally entrenched in society in the same way as in the past. Africa's leaders must be held accountable for political corruption, mismanagement, and moral decay that create conditions of restricted opportunities for women to survive, even when they are educated, as shown in the novel.

Adichie's Pan-African sentiments are vividly conveyed in *Americanah* as a compelling issue in the African diaspora. Chapter 4 is an insightful engagement with Adichie's perceptions of African identity in the diaspora that complements other works analyzed in the book. Some observer's question the concept's viability in the global age, especially since there are collisions and fissures in the relationships between the old and new African diasporas in America and in other international spaces. In the USA, a further complication of identity is the competition for academic resources and other opportunities for ethnic minorities in America. Adichie unfolds her rejection of the seductive tendency to embrace calcified perceptions of 'difference' between African migrants born on the continent and African-descended communities in the diaspora, articulated as 'learning to be black'. The historical and cultural cleavages caused by the Atlantic slave trade are indeed real and have never been resolved or healed. These dichotomies are symptomatic of the root cause of difficult relationships between African migrants and African Americans. An important strength of *Americanah* is Adichie's expressions of solidarity with African Americans as well as other African nationals, illustrated by the scene in the hair-braiding salon with her African sisters.

Literary Pan-Africanism is an innovative theoretical construct that unravels the ways in which Adichie's skillfully crafted blog engages controversial issues of identity and intra-racial dynamics among people of color. An important strength of Pan-African aesthetics is the unpacking of America's dark legacy of slavery that permeates racial encounters. Adichie's courage should be lauded given the controversial and provocative nature of these divisive energies that are sources of continued debate. The image and representation of African American characters in *Americanah* are positive, as illustrated in the character of Blaine, Ifemelu's boyfriend, who is a polished professor at Princeton.

Adichie's rejection of Afropolitanism is interesting since her life embodies the features of the term. She is highly educated, globally mobile and savvy, and a public intellectual. In the novel, Ifemelu's evolution from a struggling and isolated migrant to a self-assured professional heightens the feminist expression in the novel. Especially satisfying is her decision to return home as a reconciliation of her hybrid status, self-acceptance, and empowered Nigerian woman.

Sefi Atta's portrayal of Adeola evokes Afropolitan energies in *A Bit of Difference* (see Chapter 8). Like Ifemelu, she is educated with the mobility to travel because of her employment. The work spans multi-local sites of Nigeria, London, and America and from each vantage point her reflections unleash discomfort and alienation in London. Her life in England offers refuge from pressure to marry by her relatives in Lagos. Like Adichie's Ifemelu in *Americanah*, Adeola returns to Nigeria at the end of the novel. Returning to Nigeria is a recurring motif that signals fulfillment of nostalgic sentiments experienced by African diaspora subjects.

As a complement to the important changes in the development of the African novel, the short story genre is also undergoing a shift toward engagement with diasporic themes. In 2013, *African Literature Today* published *Writing Africa in the Short Story* to mark renewed interest in the genre. In the editorial essay, Ernest Emenyonu notes increased publication of short fiction by contemporary writers: "The younger generation of African writers in particular, have used the short story to comment on various aspects of life in modern African societies: the senselessness of violence, war, religious bigotry, racism, corruption and all forms of injustice meted to any group especially women and the disenfranchised 'others' in Africa as anywhere else in the world" (2013: 6). *West African Women in the Diaspora* interrogates short stories from three authors: Ama Aidoo, Atta Sefi, and Chimamanda Ngozi Adichie. The stories in Ama Ata Aidoo's *Diplomatic Pounds* (2012) foreground the local and global tensions of dislocated Ghanaian women who have assimilated European culture and ruptured their ties to Ghana. The stories are tales of confusion, self-denial and contested identities of women who have lived in London for decades. The women have acquired the peculiarities of Dubosian aesthetics and memory of Ghana is filtered through the foggy recollections of their families and communities in Ghana. Chapter 5 on Aidoo's collection highlights the post-colonial elements that vividly resonate with Sisi's 'Black-eyed Squint' in *Our Sister Killjoy*. The stories demonstrate a continuation of Aidoo's post-colonial gaze to query the disaffected behaviors and attitudes she observes among London-based Ghanaians. The stories evoke Aidoo's penchant for humor and irony as women characters are mere caricatures of local Ghanaians or, more succinctly, shadows of their former (African) selves. All the women characters experience some form of dysphoria and seek their cultural moorings in London, rather than Ghana as homeland. Fragmented identity links all the stories as a chronicle of African women who are 'lost' in the diaspora.

Taiye Selasi's *Ghana Must Go* received critical reception as a successful work of diaspora expression (see Chapter 6). The vivid portrayal of splintered emotions of a Nigerian–Ghanaian family is displayed in multi-local sites of America, Nigeria, and Ghana. Diasporic nostalgia haunts the novel as the tensions between the characters are played out against frazzled relationships and the search for stability in their lives. In this novel, the idea of 'return' is a recurring motif as an important feature of immigrant fiction. Sadly, the hopes and dreams of the family members are frustrated by the convoluted experiences in America and for the siblings in Nigeria. The structure of the work skillfully unveils the potential for trauma and estrangement amidst debilitating challenges in the diaspora space of America as well as in Nigeria for the children. The characters have potential for Afropolitan lifestyles, but their success is marred by a complexity of social and cultural forces.

Sefi Atta's "News from Home" and "A Temporary Position" and Adichie's "On Monday of last Week" frame the act of 'gazing' as a constantly shifting process of inner reflection on notions of 'here' and 'elsewhere' (see Chapter 7). In all the stories, the tensions that arise within each female character leads to critique of Nigeria and the choices she made when she was home. In the same way as other writers examined in this book, post-colonial perspectives on problems in Nigeria claim their attention, but unlike Unigwe's women characters, the women are educated. In "A Temporary Position" and "News from Home", the women realize that no matter how uncomfortable they are in the West, the problems in Nigeria are worse and they will not return. Of all the works explored, *Americanah* and *There's No Place Like Home* hold more promise than others for reconciliation of diaspora angst for women migrants.

For some African women, the transnational 'gaze' provides clarity, purpose, a stronger sense of identity, and the possibility of renewed cultural ties. Despite the uncertain trajectories of developing nations in Africa, migration is not always the solution, as illustrated in the vibrant mix of African diaspora fiction. Ideas of 'return' to Africa form an elliptical arc to connect contemporary writers with Emecheta and

Aidoo who queried their people over the choice to remain abroad in their classic diaspora works, *Second Class Citizen* and *Our Sister Killjoy* respectively.

African literary history is being rewritten by a constellation of women authors whose new stories mirror new landscapes of identity in the twenty-first century. Diaspora narratives command attention to pressing issues that haunt the lives of African émigrés as borderland subjects. By connecting the past to realities of diaspora life, women transform the meaning of being African. If the twentieth century belongs to African male writers through the production of post-colonial classics, it is also true that African women have reclaimed their creative fiction from the margins to dominate robust production of successful and compelling works.

Works cited

Adichie. Chimamanda Ngozi. *Americanah*. New York. Alfred A. Knopf. 2013.
Aidoo, Ama Ata. *Our Sister Killjoy: Or Reflections of a Black-Eyed Squint*. New York. Longman. 1977.
——— *Diplomatic Pounds*. London. Ayebia Clarke Publishing. 2012.
Atta. Sefi. *News From Home*. Northampton. Interlink Books. 2009.
Emecheta. Buchi. *Second Class Citizen*. New York. George Braziller. 1974.
Emenyonu, Ernest. *Writing Africa in the Short Story*. *African Literature Today*. Vol. 31. Suffolk. James Currey. 2013. pp. 1–7.
Feldner, Maximillian. *Narrating the New Diaspora: 21st century Nigerian Literature in Context*. Switzerland. Palgrave Macmillan. 2019.
Gyasi. Yaa. *Homegoing*. New York. Vintage Books. 2016.
———. *Transcendent Kingdom*. New York. Alfred. A. Knopf. 2020.
Habila, Helon. "The Future of African Literature". *The Journal of the African Literature Association*. Vol. 13. No. 1. 2019. pp. 153–162.
Quayson, Ato. "Modern African Literary History: Nation, and Narration, Orality and Diaspora". *The Journal of the African Literature Association*. Vol. 13. No. 1. 2019. pp. 131–150.
Selasi, Taiye. *Ghana Must Go*. New York. The Penguin Press. 2013.

Index

Abani, C. 2, 42
Achebe, C. 1, 42, 54, 85
Adah's Story 15
Adichie, C. N. 3, 13, 40, 42, 106, 128; on Afropolitanism 63–64, 93–94, 128; on the Atlantic slave trade 61; on being *black* in America 54–58; on challenges of hybridity for immigrants 91; critical acclaim for 53–54; education of 53; on impact of racial difference on African women traveling abroad 30; literary corpus of 53–54; on longing and return home 87; Pan-Africanism and 8–10, 58–65; radical feminist works by 20; short story genre and 68, 98–99; as third-generation writer 85; on the transnational gaze 107–108; on women's emotional dilemmas and loneliness 108–109; *see also Americanah*; *News from Home*; *Thing Around Your Neck, The*
Adua 85
African and American: West Africans in Post-Civil Rights America 115
African Literature Today 68, 99, 128
Africanness 2, 62
African self 2, 87
Afropolitanism 5–7, 62–64, 84, 88, 92–95, 128
After the Ceremonies 27
Aidoo, A. A. 1, 3, 5, 9, 24, 108, 111, 126, 128–129; experimentation with positionality 80; as feminist writer 28; as godmother of Anglophone African women's fiction 27; literary corpus of 27; post-colonial writing by 67–68, 78; return to literary stage in 2012 67; on transnational gaze 129–130; *see also Changes, a Love Story*; *Diplomatic Pounds & Other Stories*; *Our Sister Killjoy or Reflections of a Black-Eyed Squint*
Amadi, E. 85
Americanah 8, 13, 30, 42, 85, 87, 112, 114, 126; on African immigrants 56–57, 91–92; on *blackness* in America 54–55; on discourse of race and identity through lens of gender 55–56; Pan-Africanism and 58–60, 127–128
Angry Letter in January, An 27
Anowa 27, 69
Armah, A. K. 3
Arndt, S. 19, 20, 33
assimilation and acculturation 72–73
Atta, S. 3, 10, 13, 40, 42, 68, 85, 128; Afropolitanism and 128; "A Temporary Position" 100–101; on impact of racial difference on African women traveling abroad 30, 98; on longing and returning home 87; on outcomes for women battling adversity 41; on sexual abuse of children 92; on the transnational gaze 99; on women struggling in challenging Nigerian environment 101–106; *see also*

Bit of Difference, A; "News from Home"
Awoonor, K. 3
Ayim, N. O. 3, 13, 28, 85

Ba, M. 5, 24
Bady, A. 55
Behold the Dreamers 13
Better Never than Late 14, 40, 100
Birds and Other Poems 27
Bit of Difference, A 10, 13, 30, 85, 87, 128; on brain drain in Africa 118–120; on immigrant experience abroad 112–119; NGO work explored in 117–119; promise of new life at end of 121–122; on racialization of Africans in the US and UK 115–117; on women's loneliness abroad 120–121
Black Messiah, The 40
blackness 27, 32, 86; in America 54–58, 61, 126
Born in Nigeria 40
Boyce-Davies, C. 103
Bride Price, The 14
Bulawayo, N. 13, 40, 85, 114
Busia, A. 3
Bye Bye Babar 5–6, 93

Changes, a Love Story 5, 27, 35, 68, 111
Chopin, K. 81
Clifford, J. 73
colonial mentality 35
colonization 28, 29, 30, 36
Concubine, The 85
Conrad, J. 30
crisis of identity 71–72
cultural identity 71–72

Dangaremgba, T. T. 72, 114
Darko, A. 3
Dash, R. K. 75
Daswani, G. 87
Davies, C. B. 17
Dear Ijeawelwe or: A Feminist Manifesto in Fifteen Suggestions 54
Death and the Kings Horseman 1
Destination Biafra 14
Dilemma of a Ghost, The 27, 69

Diplomatic Pounds & Other Stories 9, 27, 67–68, 99, 111, 128; on assimilation and acculturation 72–73; on complex interplay between individuals 78–82; crisis of identity in 71–72; "Diplomatic Pounds" 74–76, 82; "Funnyless" 72–74, 82; gendered lens in 69; metanarrative of diaspora in 81–82; "Mixed Messages" 76–78, 82; "New Lessons" 69–73, 82; on obsession 74–76; on perceptions of home 74; post-colonial literary theory and 68–69; "Rain" 78–82; spatio-temporal dimensions in 70–71; on women's perceptions of themselves and each other 76–78
double-consciousness 70
Double Yoke 14
Dubois, W.E.B. 70, 72
Dunton, C. 42–43
Dynamics of African Feminism: Defining and Classifying African Feminist Literatures, The 19–20

Eagle and the Chickens and Other Stories, The 27
Echoes in the Mind 100
Efuru 5
Eke, M. 77
Ekwensi, C. 42, 85
El Saadawi, N. 20
Emecheta, B. 1, 3, 5, 7, 111, 126; autobiographical writing of 16–17; contemporaries of 13–14; criticism of the honesty and courage of 17; on the double yoke 19; feminist themes in writing of 14–17; literary corpus of 14–15; loss of social class in London 21–22; on otherness 18, 24; prizes awarded to 15; on survival through sisterhood 22–23; writing from woman's perspective 15–16; *see also In the Ditch*; *Second Class Citizen*
Emenyonu, E. 2, 99
Evaristo, B. 14, 85, 100
Everything Good Will Come 42, 101
Eze, C. 93
Ezeigbo, A. A. 41, 100, 111

Index 133

Feldner, M. 86, 88, 99, 125
"Female Writer and Her Commitment, The" 5
"Feminist Impulse and Social Realism in Ama Ata Aidoo's *No Sweetness Here* and *Our Sister Killjoy*" 35
feminist writing 5, 14–17, 28, 36, 124; on patriarchy 19–21, 28; radical 19–20; self-actualization in 23
Foreign Gods 88
Fractures and Fragments 100
Frank, K. 23, 37
"Funnyless" 72–74, 82

Gerhmann, S. 63
Ghana Must Go 9, 13, 28, 129; Afropolitanism in 94–95; identity confusion and disconnection in 90–91; longing for home as theme of 88, 95–96; narrative structure of 86; on *otherness* 86–87; sexual abuse of children in 89; three sections of 84–85; women's life choices examined in 88–89
Ghanian writers 3, 7–9, 28, 67–68, 125
Gikandi, S. 6, 63, 93
Girl, Woman Other 14, 85, 100
Girl Who Can and Other Stories, The 27, 99
God Child, The 13, 28, 85
God Dies by the Nile 20
Goyal, Y. 115
Graceland 42
Gyasi, Y. 3, 13, 28, 40, 85, 125

Habila, H. 98–99, 124
Hagan, J. 47
Half of a Yellow Sun 53
Hall, S. 4, 70–72, 74, 114
Halter, M. 115
Hassan, S. 93
Head Above Water 15, 16, 85
Heart of Darkness 30
home, perceptions of 74
Homegoing 13, 28, 85, 87, 125

In Search of the Afropolitan: Encounters, Conversations, and Contemporary Diasporic African Literature 6
Interpreters, The 42
In the Ditch 1, 5, 7, 13–17, 20–24, 28, 85, 111; on loss of social class 21–22; patriarchy in 20–21; survival through sisterhood in 22–23

Jagua Nana 42, 85
Jagua Nana's Daughter 85
Johnson, V. 115
Joys of Motherhood, The 14, 15, 42
Jyothirmai, D. 98

Kehinde 1, 5, 15
Kigotho, W. 61–62
Kind of Marriage, A 15
Knudsen, E. R. 6

Lagoon 42
Lion and the Jewel, The 1, 85
Literary Pan-Africanism: History, Contexts, and Criticism 58

Magic Breast Bags 100
Makokha, J. K. S. 6
Mbue, I. 13
Migraine-George, T. 69
"Mixed Messages" 76–78, 82
Modernity, an Introduction to Modern Societies 4, 114
Moonlight Bride, The 14

Naira Power 14–15
Narrating the New African Diaspora: twenty-first Literature in Context 99, 125
Ndibe, O. 88
Negotiating Afropolitanism: Essays on Borders and Spaces in Contemporary African Literature and Folklore 6, 93
neocolonialism 28, 31
neoliberalism 50
Nervous Conditions 72–73, 114
"New Lessons" 69–73, 82
"News from Home" 10, 41–42, 68, 92, 99, 103–106, 109, 112, 129

New Tribe, The 1, 15
New Women's Writing in African Literature 2
Nigerian independence from Britain 42
Nigerian writers 3, 7–10, 42–43, 125
Night Dancer 40
Noah, T. 60
No Longer at Ease 42
No Sweetness Here 27, 68, 99
Nowhere to Play 14
Nwankwo, C. 35
Nwapa, F. 3, 5, 24

obsession 74–76
Odamtten, V. 29, 68, 77
Ogudipe-Leslie, M. 5, 16, 82
Ojaide, T. 70
Okorafor, N. 42
Olaniyi, R. 44
On Black Sister's Street 8, 13, 41–51, 85, 87, 100, 111, 126–127; as cautionary tale 41; hybrid identities in 41–42; realism in 44; tragic end to 47–48; violence and sex trafficked women in 43–50
"On Monday of Last Week" 108–109
otherness 18, 37, 78, 91; development of personhood in 24; trauma of 86–87; women breaking barriers of 62; women's initiation into 14, 28–30
Our Sister Killjoy or Reflections of a Black-Eyed Squint 1, 7–8, 27–37, 67–69, 108, 111, 128, 130; blackness in 27, 32; collective "oppositional" gaze in 36; feminism in 36; friendship in 31–33; otherness in 27, 30, 37; sections of 28–29; victimhood trope of 31, 33–34

Pahl, M. 56
Pan-Africanism 8–9, 53, 58–65, 127–128
Parkes, N. A. 3
patriarchy 19–21, 28
People of the City 42
Phoenix 40

"Politics of Exile: Reflections of a Black-Eyed Squint in *Our Sister Killjoy*, The" 29
Porter, A. 20
post-colonial writing 2–4, 35, 50, 54, 67–69, 78, 98, 124
"Private Selves and Public Spaces: Autobiography and the African Woman Writer" 17
Purple Hibiscus 20, 42, 53, 54, 62

Quayson, A. 87, 125

radical feminist writing 19–20
Rahbek, U. 6
"Rain" 78–82
Ramesh, S. 98
Rape of Shavi, The 15
Recreating Ourselves: African Women and Critical Transformations 16
Reese, H. 60
Rhythm of Life 100
Rituals and Departures 100

Sackeyfio, R. 35, 43, 56–57, 100, 101
Scego, I. 85
Second Class Citizen 1, 5, 7, 13–24, 28, 85, 130; patriarchy in 19–20; racism in 18–19
Selasi, T. 3, 5–6, 9, 13, 28, 40, 125, 129; on Afropolitanism 62–63; Afropolitanism and 94–95; narrative structure used by 86; as third-generation writer 85; see also *Ghana Must Go*
self-representation, narrative 17
sex trafficking/sex workers 43–50, 111, 126–127
sexual abuse of children 89
short story genre 68, 98–100
Sizemore, C. 19
Slave Girl, The 14, 15
So Long a Letter 5
Someone Talking to Sometime 27
Sougou, O. 22, 76
Souls of Blackfolk, The 72
Southerland, E. 3
Soyinka, W. 1, 42, 85
Storr, J. 64
Swallow 41, 42, 101

Tear Drops 40
Temple, C. N. 8, 53, 58, 64
"Temporary Position, A" 100–101, 106, 109
"Temporary Position, A" 129
Thing Around Your Neck, The 54, 68, 85, 87, 99, 106, 111, 114
Things Fall Apart 1, 85
third-generation African women's writing 40–41, 54, 85, 125
Titch the Cat 14
Trafficked 41
Transcendent Kingdom 28, 125
transnational gaze 98, 99, 107, 129–130

Umeh, M. 15, 16, 22
Unigwe, C. 3, 8, 13–14, 51, 85, 87, 100, 126–127; literary corpus of 40; as third-generation African writer 40–41; *see also On Black Sister's Street*

wa Nguhi, M. 2
Wawrzinek, J. 6
We Need New Names 85, 114
We Should All Be Feminists 54

West African women's diasporic writing: Afropolitanism in 5–7, 62–64, 84, 88, 92–95, 128; feminist (*see* feminist writing); fiction 1, 11; fiction of 2–3; narratives of 1–2; Pan-Africanism in 8–9, 53, 58–65, 127–128; post-colonial 2–4, 35, 54, 67–69, 78, 98, 124; prominent writers of 3, 13–14, 111–112; remembrance and return to homeland in writing on 87–88; shifting identities in 2, 4, 41–42, 62, 67–68, 69, 70, 85–86, 114–115; short story genre in 68, 98–100; stereotypical roles of women explored in 85; third-generation writers in 40–41, 54, 85, 125; transnational gaze in 98, 99
Wilentz, G. 29
Wilson-Tagoe, N. 2
Woman at Point Zero 20
"Women Without Men: The Feminist Novel in Africa" 23
Wrestling Match, The 14
Writing Africa in Short Story 68, 99, 128

Yang, H. 29, 69

Taylor & Francis eBooks

www.taylorfrancis.com

A single destination for eBooks from Taylor & Francis with increased functionality and an improved user experience to meet the needs of our customers.

90,000+ eBooks of award-winning academic content in Humanities, Social Science, Science, Technology, Engineering, and Medical written by a global network of editors and authors.

TAYLOR & FRANCIS EBOOKS OFFERS:

- A streamlined experience for our library customers
- A single point of discovery for all of our eBook content
- Improved search and discovery of content at both book and chapter level

REQUEST A FREE TRIAL
support@taylorfrancis.com

For Product Safety Concerns and Information please contact our EU representative GPSR@taylorandfrancis.com
Taylor & Francis Verlag GmbH, Kaufingerstraße 24, 80331 München, Germany